Your Life Savings on Steroids

Warren Sterling

Contents

YOUR LIFE SAVINGS ON STEROIDS

CRITICAL DISCLAIMERS

This guidebook is published solely for informational and educational purposes and is not, and should not be construed as, personalized investment, tax, or legal advice.

- **RISK WARNING**: Investing in Exchange-Traded Funds (ETFs) involves significant risk, including the risk of losing your entire principal investment. Past performance is not an indicator of future results.
- **APP DISCLOSURE: EDUCATIONAL TOOL ONLY**
    - The referenced investment assistant tools (downloadable files and web application) are practice and simulation tools designed to help you follow along with the concepts in this book.
    - It does **not** provide personalized investment advice, brokerage services, or buy/sell recommendations. Trade alerts are designed as a market-wide, portfolio-level timing signals and not a recommendation to buy or sell a specific security. Portfolio positions are se-

lected and traded by the users in their own brokerage accounts. **These tools do not execute trades on behalf of their users**.

- The author and publisher are not responsible for the performance, accuracy, errors, or output of the provided tools, nor for any investment losses incurred through its use.

- **YOUR RESPONSIBILITY**: You are solely responsible for your own investment decisions. You must consult with a qualified, licensed financial, tax, and/or legal professional before making any investment choices. The author and publisher assume no liability for any losses or damages incurred as a result of using the information contained herein.

- For the **full legal disclosure** please refer to the appendix section at the end of the book.

- **COPYRIGHT**: All rights reserved. No part of this book may be reproduced in any form or by any electronic or mechanical means, including information storage and retrieval systems, without written permission from the author, except for the use of brief quotations in a book review.

- Published by **ETF4Life LLC**[1], a California company.

- All other trademarks are the property of their respective owners.

Introduction

What **this guide is not**: this guide is not a manual for short-term trading strategies. It won't teach you how to trade individual company stocks or derivatives, nor will it recommend specific company stocks to buy or sell.

What this guide is: this guide will demonstrate and explain a **methodical approach to optimizing your long-term savings' performance** using Exchange Traded Funds (ETFs). It will show how this approach has the potential to considerably outperform traditional savings and investment strategies.

The Principles Discussed in This Book

A Proven Concept and How to Replicate It (Chapters 6 & 8)

- **Top Performance**: Demonstrating a **three-fold** increase in value in six years, beating top professionally managed funds and all major market indices.
- **Persistence**: How to use the model on your own while **staying invested** for a greater compounding effect.

- **Top-Down Precision:** Trade alerts triggered by market-wide indicators rather than the "noise" of individual stocks.
- **Supervised Autopilot**: An app-based system that streamlines the process, reducing your time commitment to trade execution.

Key Lessons from the U.S. Financial Markets (Chapters 1, 3 & 7)

- **Inherent Growth Trajectory**: The U.S. stock market has a fundamental nature of **exponential growth** driven by productivity, innovation, and global capital.
- **The Business Cycle**: The stock market experiences occasional periods of weakness that sometimes manifest as a severe value erosion, known as a "correction" or a "bear market".
- **The "Policy Put"**: Central banks and governments intervene with supportive policies during severe downturns, effectively providing a safety net for asset prices.

Investment Approach (Chapters 3, 4 & 5)

- **The Contrarian Investor**: How corrections and bear-markets are leveraged to considerably enhance long-term portfolios growth.
- **The World's Strongest Growth Engine**: Why the **technology sector** is an ideal resource for accelerating investments growth potential due to high margins and disruptive potential in areas like AI, cloud computing, and robotics.

- **The Power of ETFs**: How carefully selected ETFs are used in conjunction with this contrarian strategy to achieve built-in diversification.
- **The Long-Short Time Horizon**: How a long-term framework translates into short and mid-term benefits.

Risk Management (Chapters 1, 3 & 5)

- **The real market risk** is NOT its drop in value.
- **The Advantage Play**: The selected ETFs' correlation with the technology sector, combined with their built-in diversification and a contrarian strategy, can turn brutal corrections into a **strong value growth opportunity**.

Investor Education (Chapters 2, 7, Appendices A & B)

- Traditional financial instruments and strategies.
- The U.S. economy, economic policy, economic indicators and their importance.

What Will I Get from This Book?

This book will provide you with both the background information and **bias awareness** necessary to help you build the understanding and confidence in this approach, free from the fear associated with stock market price fluctuations. I'll then offer a **system you can follow for years to come**, along with the rationale behind its various parameters.

The book includes a **case-study** section, where the model's performance is evaluated using years of real market data taken from technology sector ETFs' price action. Finally, a **step-by-step guide** will walk you through setting up and using the system on your own with the help of our Excel and web-based **trade alert tools**[2], thereby streamlining your decision-making process.

- You'll be in full control of your funds and your privacy. Our tools will not link to your brokerage account.

How Will This Model Fit into My Existing Assets Mix?

The model's strong performance potential should begin to materialize over a period of a few months to a year, becoming more pronounced over time, as shown in the case study later in the book. As such, it can be an excellent fit for the **stock portion in a diversified retirement savings account** (or any other long-term investment plan). For example, in a traditional 60/40 mix of stocks to bonds, the 60% stock slice could be based on this model.

Not Expecting to Retire Soon but Actively Saving?

This model has the potential to serve you very well and become a major part of your lifelong financial plan, addressing many of your long-term goals. It is designed to portray the concepts and habits required for making your long-term investment journey successful. The model could also benefit those looking for robust **short-to-mid-term strategies within a long-term framework**. For more on that check out "The Surprising Aspect of Long-Term Investing" later in the book.

Unlike Some Other Systems, This Investment Model:

- Provides ample liquidity[3] and diversification[4].

- In its basic form, does not involve picking and managing individual stocks.

- Does not involve betting on short term directionality.

- Uses a **top-down approach**, where trades are triggered by market-wide events and by portfolio-level indicators. The calculated trade amounts are first allocated to the portfolio as a whole and then broken down to the individual positions based on their assigned weights.

- The app can be used for **paper trading**[5].

- The app will **not** execute automated trades directly in your brokerage account. This will keep you involved while protecting your privacy.

- Does not require a high net worth or high income.

- Is entirely self-managed, saving on fees and maximizing flexibility.

- Is designed to outperform the sectors or index mix it is based on.

- Fits into traditional savings models, such as the 60/40 stocks to bonds.

The model, in its **investment assistant** form, is implemented as a web application. It takes in basic portfolio information along with real-time market data and apply AI-defined triggers and weights to generate timely buy or sell trade alerts. A trade alert will post the **trade amount** for the portfolio as a whole and also the calculated amounts for each of its positions based on the user-assigned relative weights. The purpose is to **streamline** market analysis and help focus investor efforts on executing the actual trades. Consider it your "**supervised autopilot**".

- The model can also be self-managed manually without the app. A guideline is available in Appendix C.

General Disclaimers

1. **Trading is not an exact science.** The stock market does not adhere to strict rules of how much it will move in any given direction, nor does any individual equity. Therefore, it's crucial to combine a robust quantitative model, which serves as a guide, with the

development of your own market intuition. Identifying opportunities - such as when, what and how much to buy or sell - will require practice and should build over time as you use this model.

2. **This is not a "get rich quick" pitch, nor is getting "rich" the goal of this guide**. Instead, maintaining a sustained growth portfolio over long periods of time (months to years) is, in the author's opinion, the safest and most enduring method for most individuals to profit from the stock market.

3. **This guidebook contains many financial and economic terms**, most of which are explained in the text and in the appendices at the end. However, since this is not an "economy 101" guide, the explanations here are merely attempted at what's necessary to understand the concepts around which the model is built. More information can be found by searching online and by tuning-in to business-related broadcasts such as CNBC, Fox Business Network or Bloomberg TV.

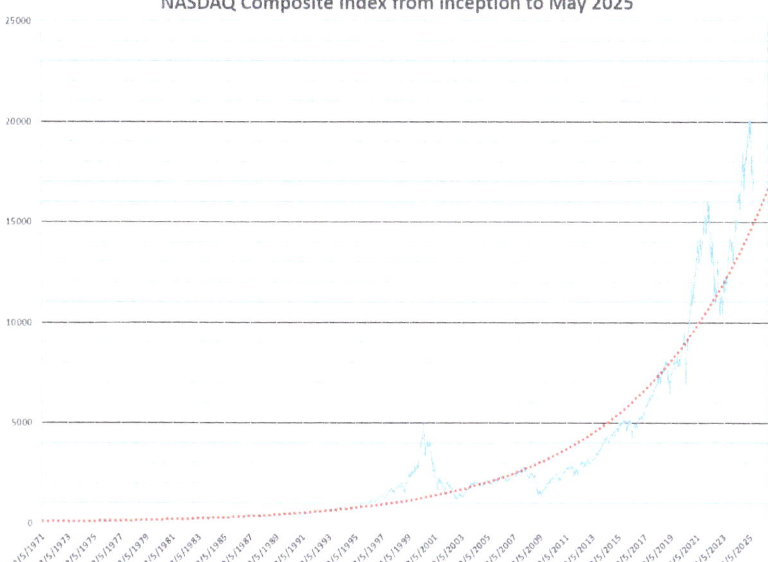

About the Author

Warren Sterling is a retired computer engineering manager and Silicon Valley veteran who brings decades of analytical precision to his work as an active portfolio manager across stocks, ETFs, and cryptocurrencies. As the creator of the **ETF4Life** model, he leverages his technical background to provide investors with the quantitative "supervised autopilot" systems necessary to navigate market volatility with confidence.

Chapter 1. Rethinking Risk

"The bottom is when your uncle calls you asking if they should be getting out." – Market Wisdom

"Volatility is not risk. It's opportunity." – Charlie Munger

1.1 The Big Picture

Stock market risk is an inherent characteristic of investing, representing the possibility that an investment's actual return will differ from its expected return, often resulting in a loss of capital. It encompasses a broad spectrum of uncertainties, from the volatility[6] of individual company shares to broader economic downturns. However, while the word "risk" often carries a negative connotation, it's crucial to understand that these very challenges are inextricably linked to the opportunities for significant growth and returns that the stock market offers.

At its core, stock market risk manifests in several forms. **Market risk**, also known as systematic risk, refers to the risk of losses due to factors affecting the entire market, such as recessions, interest rate changes, or geopolitical events. It cannot be diversified away. Then there's **specific risk** (or unsystematic risk), which is unique to a particular company or industry, such as a product recall, management changes, or new competition. This type of risk can often be mitigated through diversification[7] across different companies and sectors. Other risks include **liquidity risk**, where an investor might not be able to sell an asset quickly enough without significantly impacting its price, and **inflation risk**, where the purchasing power of investment returns is eroded over time by rising prices.

Despite these potential pitfalls, risk is the very engine of opportunity in the financial markets. The possibility of losing money is precisely why investors demand a higher return for taking on greater risk. For instance, during periods of market downturns, when panic selling drives down stock prices, value investors see an opportunity to acquire quality assets at a discount. What appears to be a severe risk to short-term holders can be a long-term bargain for those with patience and a discerning eye. Similarly, investing in innovative, high-growth companies carries a higher specific risk due to their nascent nature, but also offers the potential for exponential returns if their ventures succeed.

Furthermore, managing risk effectively can unlock opportunities. Through strategies like **diversification**, investors spread their capital across various asset classes, industries, and geographies, reducing the impact of poor performance in any single investment. Another common strategy for mitigating risk while enhancing profits during such times is **dip buying**, which involves purchasing shares of a stock or an index-tracking ETF after it experienced a temporary decline in price.

1.2 The Stock Market "Put"

In the realm of financial markets, a "put" option grants its holder the right, but not the obligation, to sell an underlying asset at a specified "strike price" on or before a certain expiration date. It serves as a form of insurance, allowing investors to limit potential losses if the asset's price falls. When discussing policymakers and their response to deteriorating financial conditions, the concept of a "stock market put" or, more specifically, a **"Fed put"** or "Greenspan put," takes on a broader, metaphorical meaning. It signifies the widespread market belief that central banks or governments will intervene with supportive **monetary or fiscal policies**[8] to prevent severe financial market downturns or economic crises, effectively providing a "safety net" for asset prices.

This implicit "put" arises from the expectation that policymakers will not allow a sustained, significant decline in asset values, fearing the contagion effect on the broader economy. If financial conditions deteriorate rapidly, potentially leading to a credit crunch, widespread bankruptcies, or a collapse in confidence, central banks might lower **interest rates**[9], inject liquidity into the financial system, or engage in quantitative easing. Similarly, governments might deploy fiscal measures like tax cuts, increased spending, or direct stimulus to prop up demand and stabilize markets. The idea is that such interventions limit the "downside risk" for investors, much like a put option.

1.3 "This Time is Different" – is it Really?

This saying is often used when a new economic, geopolitical or other crisis looms, and the stock market starts to descend sharply. This sounds believable for a while because the source of the new trouble looks and feels different, making it seem like we're in uncharted territory, a new paradigm that may lead to cataclysmic outcomes.

It turns out there's always a "put" somewhere that saves the day.

Fed puts:

- The 1987 Stock Market Crash (Black Monday): Following the unprecedented 22.6% single-day drop in the Dow Jones Industrial Average on October 19, 1987, the Fed (short for the Federal Reserve), under chairman Alan Greenspan, quickly intervened. They issued a statement assuring liquidity to the banking system and subsequently lowered interest rates. This swift action is widely credited with preventing a deeper financial crisis and reinforced the perception that the Fed would act as a backstop for the market.

- The Asian Financial Crisis and Russian Debt Default (1998): In the face of global financial turmoil stemming from the Asian financial crisis and the Russian sovereign debt default, the Fed again lowered interest rates unexpectedly. This move was seen as a proactive measure to prevent these international crises from severely impacting the U.S. financial system and further cemented the "Greenspan Put" notion.

- The Dot-Com Bubble Burst (2000-2002): As the internet bubble deflated and stock markets plummeted, the Fed embarked on a series of aggressive interest rate cuts to stimulate the economy and cushion the blow to financial markets.

Fiscal puts:

- The Great Depression and the New Deal (1930s): In response to the unprecedented economic collapse of the Great Depression, President Franklin D. Roosevelt's "New Deal" program involved massive government spending on public works projects, social welfare programs, and financial reforms. While not solely aimed at propping up stock prices, these fiscal policies were designed to stimulate demand, create jobs, and restore confidence in the financial system, thereby laying a floor under economic activity and indirectly supporting asset values.

- The 2008 Global Financial Crisis and Stimulus Packages: In the wake of the 2008 financial crisis, governments worldwide implemented substantial fiscal stimulus packages. In the U.S., the American Recovery and Reinvestment Act of 2009 was a significant example, directing hundreds of billions of dollars towards infrastructure, tax cuts, and aid to states. This fiscal intervention was intended to prevent a deeper recession, stabilize financial markets, and restore aggregate demand. Similarly, the Troubled Asset Relief Program (TARP) involved direct government intervention to purchase distressed assets from financial institutions, preventing widespread bank failures and a complete meltdown of the financial system.

Similar interventions occurred in every crisis in the last 100 years, whether big or small. They can be carried out by either direct or indirect action, such as a statement or a tweet. In every pullback, experienced investors are always on the look for signs of the next "put". The prospects of people losing their life savings can therefore materialize only if they panic and head to the exits prematurely, or if they don't diversify sufficiently (e.g., by putting all of their savings in a stock of a single company that goes bust).

1.4 Volatility Is Our Counter-Intuitive Friend

We are taught to seek stability, to avoid unnecessary risk, and so, instinctively, we view market turbulence as an enemy to be avoided. Yet, for the long-term investor, this conventional wisdom is profoundly misguided. Volatility, counter-intuitively, is not our foe but rather a powerful, albeit disguised, friend.

Volatility can manifest in downward as well as upward moves in stock prices.

The reasons for volatility in the stock market range from shaky economic predictions, missed earnings results, illiquidity, political instability and geopolitical tensions, financial sector distress, herd mentality and greed, to plain old profit-taking, leading to healthy pullbacks. These factors often interact in complex ways, making precise predictions of market movements impossible. Volatility is a natural and inherent characteristic of financial markets.

This unavoidable volatility can manifest itself in various magnitudes and time periods. It is when it goes to the extreme that it can many times signal a **trading opportunity**. The model described later in the book uses the **VIX** (the CBOE Volatility Index), along with other indicators to generate buy signals. The VIX is often also called "the fear gauge". When it moves significantly above its multi-year average, it usually indicates a heightened investor nervousness and tends to align with strong stock market movements. With VIX at extremely high levels, the major market indices typically move down sharply, sometimes by a few percentage points in a single trading day, creating an opportunity to buy the lows, which turns risk into opportunity.

1.5 What's the Real Risk, then?

"Risk is not having the money you need when you need it." – Charles Ellis

Playing the long game, responding to corrections in a measured way and diversifying properly are the pillars of effective risk mitigation and profit generation. The real risk, or more accurately, the unknown, is **time**. Bear markets[10] in particular can last for extended periods. In recent economic recessions[11] it took anything from a few months to over two years for the stock market to recover its losses. Recessions are not common but are still an unavoidable part of the business cycle. Hence the execution of the strategy in this guidebook must account for the time it may take to emerge from such an event with a profit. This may mean ensuring **sufficient reserves** are available to buy and hold for as long as needed. If acted upon decisively during a recession, the profit outcome of the eventual recovery can be much larger than during a normal market.

1.6 What's That "Diversification" Noise All About?

The ideal diversified portfolio is a debated topic, but what's not debated is that diversification reduces the volatility of individual components, leading to a smoother and more predictable investment journey.

Historically, the stock market has had a positive long-term return, while individual stocks, on average, have had a negative return. Most stocks not only didn't maintain a consistent growth trajectory but actually experienced poor or negative long-term performance. This is despite many of them receiving a "buy" or "strong buy" rating from their respective analysts. The stocks that turned out to be big winners are in the minority. This means that retail investors owning a small number of stocks are more likely to pick losers, especially if they select their stocks early on.

How our model practices diversification

What does it take to diversify a portfolio? It involves picking dozens of individual stocks and then ranking them by their underlying business' products, industry, market cap, and many other elements, including exposure to major risk factors. This process is called "**fundamental analysis**"[12]. Then you also need to decide how much of your capital will be allocated to each of your top ranked names.

- Many investors tend to shortcut this process by picking stocks from popular headlines, friends, or worse – taking tips from social media influencers. This brings into play investor psychology[13] factors that may result in far-from-optimal performance.

Professional portfolio managers are best suited for conducting such detailed and knowledgeable work. To access these services efficiently, one can simply choose an Exchange Traded Fund (ETF)[14], which streamlines the investment process by removing the need for the elaborate individual stock selection, while providing diversification and proper weights for each of their holdings. **ETFs offer both professional risk management and targeted exposure to the market, all with lower day-to-day volatility compared to their individual constituents.**

Therefore, our model portfolio is composed of several ETFs.

ETFs come in many different flavors, each specializing in a separate stock category or sector. To achieve an even better diversification, we've selected several category ETFs to complete our cross-diversified portfolio.

The model's ETFs selection is described in detail in a later chapter.

Chapter 2. Traditional Investment Instruments

- **While this list includes many popular instruments, it does not aim to cover all existing variations.**

Asset Classes

2.1 Fixed Income: Bonds

Investing in fixed income involves purchasing debt instruments that pay a fixed stream of interest payments over a specified period, typically returning the principal at maturity. Common examples include government bonds, corporate bonds, and municipal bonds. These investments are generally considered less volatile than equities and are often favored by investors seeking stable income, capital preservation, or diversification within a portfolio. While typically offering lower returns than stocks, fixed income investments provide predictable cash flows and can act as a counterbalance during periods of market downturns. However, they are not without risk, as interest rate fluctuations can impact bond prices, and there's always the potential for default, particularly with lower-rated issuers.

Risks: interest rates; credit defaults; reinvestment (at a lower rate); liquidity risk; market risk (if sold before maturity).

Upside potential: yield in single-digit range.

2.2 Equities: Stocks

Investing in public company **stocks** means purchasing shares of individual companies, making you a partial owner. This offers the potential for significant capital appreciation if the company thrives, and some stocks also pay dividends. However, it exposes you to "single-stock risk," meaning the failure or poor performance of that one company can significantly impact your investment.

Risks: company-specific business risk; volatility due to a specific government policy or investor sentiment; liquidity risk.

Upside potential: a wide range of performance outcomes, often short term in nature.

2.3 Real Estate

Investing in real estate offers the potential for income generation through rental properties and capital appreciation as property values rise, but it often requires substantial capital, active management, and carries illiquidity risk. A more accessible alternative is investing in Real Estate Investment Trusts (REITs), which are companies that own, operate, or finance income-producing real estate. REITs trade like stocks on major exchanges, providing diversification, professional management, and regular dividend income without the direct responsibilities of property ownership.

However, both direct real estate and REIT investments are susceptible to market fluctuations, interest rate changes, and economic downturns, which can impact property values, rental income, and overall returns.

REIT risks: interest rates policy; taxation (dividends counting as ordinary income).

Upside potential: notwithstanding sensitivity to lengthy interest rate cycles, long-term annualized returns, including dividends, are typically in the range of 8% to 12%.

2.4 Cash Equivalent Assets

Investing in cash equivalent assets means holding highly liquid, short-term investments that can be readily converted into a known amount of cash with minimal risk of value change. These are often used for **immediate liquidity needs**, emergency funds, or as a temporary holding place for capital **before deploying it into other investments**. Common examples include Money Market funds, Treasury bills (T-bills) with short maturities, and high-yield savings accounts. While offering safety and stability, cash equivalents typically provide lower returns compared to other asset classes, making them less suitable for long-term growth objectives but **crucial for maintaining financial flexibility and mitigating short-term market volatility**.

Risks: inflation

Upside potential: single-digit interest return typically; high potential for use by grabbing opportunities in a weak stock market.

2.5 Commodities

Investing in commodities involves buying and selling raw materials that are essential to the global economy, such as agricultural products (wheat, corn), energy (oil, natural gas), and metals (gold, silver, copper). This asset class can offer portfolio diversification because commodity prices often move independently of stocks and bonds, and they can also act as a hedge against inflation, as their values tend to rise with the cost of goods and services. However, commodities are known for their high volatility due to factors like supply and demand imbalances, geopolitical events, and weather patterns, and they generally do not generate income like dividends or interest, meaning returns solely depend on price appreciation. Investors typically gain exposure through futures contracts, commodity-focused ETFs, or by investing in companies that produce these raw materials.

Financial instrument risks: highly leveraged[15]; high volatility; liquidity risk (for some commodities).

Upside potential: can be high in selective markets and for limited time periods.

2.6 Cryptocurrencies

Cryptocurrencies ("crypto") are widely considered an emerging and distinct asset class, particularly by institutional investors and financial experts. While it shares some characteristics with other assets, its unique features—especially its decentralized, blockchain-based technology—set it apart from traditional categories like stocks, bonds, and real estate.

Crypto's suitability as a long-term investment is a complex topic with both potential benefits and significant risks. While it offers the potential for high returns and portfolio diversification due to its historically low correlation with traditional assets like stocks and bonds, it's also a highly speculative and volatile asset class.

At the present time, crypto's largely inconsistent correlation with the NASDAQ index excludes it from the scope of this book.

Investment Strategies
2.7 Stock-Based ETFs

In contrast to individual stocks, **Exchange-Traded Funds (ETFs)** are baskets of various securities, often stocks, that trade on exchanges like individual stocks. Buying an ETF provides instant diversification across many companies, industries, or even asset classes, significantly reducing the risk associated with any single holding. While ETFs generally offer lower returns than a wildly successful individual stock, they provide a more stable and often lower-cost way to gain broad market exposure, making them a popular choice for long-term investors seeking diversification with less active management.

Stocks are historically the best performing asset class as measured by the major indices[16]' annualized performance. They are also one of the most volatile; however, as shown throughout the book, with our model we use this volatility to our advantage. When we do that using stock-based ETFs, stocks' relative performance advantage is amplified further.

ETF Risks: tracking error[17]; sector concentration risk.

Upside potential: with the right strategy, an ETF can consistently beat the performance of its related index.

- Mutual Funds, a product similar to ETFs, are priced only once at the daily close. This makes them a less flexible option, hence inferior to ETFs in the context of this guide-book. In addition, fees are relatively high, and they're also tax-inefficient (when used in a taxable account).

2.8 Dividend-Issuing Stocks

Investing in dividend stocks involves purchasing shares of companies that regularly distribute a portion of their earnings to shareholders, typically in the form of cash payments. This strategy offers investors a steady stream of income, which can be particularly appealing for retirees or those seeking passive income. Beyond the regular payouts, dividend-paying companies are often well-established and financially stable, potentially offering more resilience during market downturns and the opportunity for long-term capital appreciation. However, dividends are not guaranteed and can be cut or suspended during challenging economic times, and focusing solely on high dividend yields can sometimes lead to "yield traps" if the underlying company is struggling.

Risks: business' financial distress; dividend cuts; "yield traps"[18]; limited growth potential of the underlying business.

Upside potential: likely less than what it would have been without the burden of the dividends distributions.

2.9 Derivatives: Options and Futures

Both options and futures present an opportunity to trade an underlying stock or commodity with less than its nominal value, namely using leverage. Success in trading relies heavily on correctly predicting the direction the underlying securities will move during the lifetime of the contract, down to its expiration. In options, for instance, this is true for trading a straight option contract and applies also to different combinations and strategies. In addition, the looming expiration introduces a time component that may hurt results. Option premiums are priced to reflect current market supply and demand, where the cost to trade depends on its **implied volatility**[19], and as a result you either end up paying more when attempting a contrarian play or taking up more risk to extend the trade, limiting the upside once again. When an option contract expires at a loss, it is a real loss of the entire premium, not just on paper as for a stock or ETF where there's no expiration date. Setting up the parameters correctly in combination trades (such as a covered call, spreads etc.) requires a very careful design to maximize profit chances. These factors require a fairly high skill to make options and futures trading a reliable source of income and to make it a major part of one's investment assets.

Risks: leverage risk (may magnify losses); liquidity risk; complexity; time decay.

Upside potential: leveraged returns (limited term).

2.10 Income Investing

Focuses on generating regular cash flow from investments, often through dividend-paying stocks, bonds, or real estate investment trusts (REITs), as covered in the previous sections.

Risks: interest rates; issuer credit/default; liquidity risk; underlying asset price decline.

Upside potential (annual typical returns): single-digit.

2.11 Dollar Cost Averaging

Involves investing a fixed amount of money at regular intervals (e.g., monthly, quarterly), regardless of market fluctuations. It reduces the impact of market volatility by averaging out the purchase price over time. You buy more shares when prices are low and fewer when prices are high.

Risks: suboptimal in bull markets.

Upside potential: by its nature, will usually underperform the major stock indices.

2.12 Passive Investing: Buy and Hold

This approach involves investing in index funds or ETFs that track a broad market index (like the S&P 500) and holding them for the long term. The goal is to match market performance rather than trying to beat it. Good for beginners, long-term investors, and those who prefer a less active role.

Risks: fluctuates with the market; no downside protection or strategy; tracking errors.

Upside potential: will perform about the same or less than the index being tracked.

2.13 Active Investing: Momentum Trades

Involves more frequent buying and selling of securities to capitalize on short-term market fluctuations and trends. Momentum investors buy stocks that are trending upward, expecting them to continue rising. This method carries a higher risk, requires significant time and research, and can incur higher trading fees and taxes. Many active investors fail to consistently beat the market.

Risks: market timing; taxation cost.

Upside potential: wide range of profit to loss, typically inconsistent and uncorrelated.

2.14 Buy the Dip, Sell the Rip

Buy the Dip refers to purchasing a stock, ETF, or other asset after its price experienced a noticeable decline from its recent highs. The underlying belief is that the dip is a temporary setback, and the asset's price is likely to rebound.

Sell the Rip refers to selling an asset after its price has experienced a rapid and significant increase (a "rip" or rally). The idea here is to capitalize on the upward momentum and lock in profits before the price potentially pulls back or corrects. It's about taking gains when the market is "hot" and perhaps overbought, with the expectation that the rapid ascent is unsustainable in the short term.

Traders often use technical indicators (like moving averages, Relative Strength Index (RSI), Bollinger Bands) to identify potential dips and rips. This method thrives in volatile markets where there are clear upward and downward swings.

Risks: relies on short-lived trends

Upside potential: inconsistent. A wide range of outcomes is possible.

- The "buy the dip, sell the rip" strategy traditionally aims to profit from short-term price fluctuations. Yet, in the short run, it's quite challenging to identify a true low, as any reversal to the downside may turn quickly into an extended fall. Attempting to keep buying the dip in such a (quite common) scenario, would feel like "catching a falling knife". That's a real risk when using short-term technical analysis[20] indicators. Hence, in the context of this model, a true dip is determined in relation to a historical, long-term trendline. Although this could at times mean a slower recovery, it is more consistent and much less risky than guessing short-term moves. History shows that the market's trajectory of exponential growth has ultimately resumed every time.

2.15 Annuities

Investing in annuities involves a contract with an insurance company where you make a payment (lump sum or series of payments) in exchange for regular income streams in the future, often in retirement. Annuities come in various forms, including fixed annuities (guaranteed returns), variable annuities (tied to investment performance), and indexed annuities (returns linked to a market index). While they offer benefits like tax-deferred growth and the potential for guaranteed lifetime income, protecting against outliving your savings, they also come with complexities such as various fees (e.g., surrender charges, administrative fees, mortality and expense charges) and can be illiquid, making them a long-term commitment that requires careful consideration of individual financial goals and risk tolerance.

Risks: surrender charges and illiquidity; tax penalties; high fees and commissions; complexity risk.

Return potential: in single-digit range.

2.16 Private Equity Funds

Investing in private equity involves providing capital to companies not listed on public stock exchanges, typically through private equity firms that pool funds from institutional and high-net-worth investors. This asset class aims for significant long-term returns by acquiring (often through leveraged buyouts or investments in early-stage businesses with high growth potential), improving, and eventually selling these private companies. While private equity can offer higher returns and portfolio diversification due to its illiquid and less correlated nature with public markets, it comes with substantial risks, including a lack of liquidity (funds are typically locked up for several years), higher fees, less transparency, and the potential for complete loss of capital if the underlying businesses fail.

Risks: illiquidity; lack of transparency; highly leveraged businesses (total loss risk); high fees and expenses; capital calls timing risk; fund manager and operational risk; valuation and exit risk.

Upside potential: often higher than public market funds (illiquidity premium).

2.17 Private Credit Firms

Investing in private credit involves providing loans directly to private companies, often those that cannot or choose not to access traditional bank lending or public bond markets. These loans are typically illiquid, privately negotiated, and can offer higher yields than publicly traded debt due to a "liquidity premium" and the custom-made nature of the financing. While private credit can offer attractive income streams, portfolio diversification, and potentially lower volatility compared to public markets, it carries increased risks such as a lack of transparency, higher default potential from smaller or less established borrowers, and the inability to easily sell investments before maturity, making it primarily suitable for sophisticated investors with a long-term investment horizon.

Risks: illiquidity; credit and default risk; lack of transparency; limited lender protections; manager and execution risk; possible conflict of interest.

Upside potential: higher interest rates than in the public markets (lower double-digit range).

2.18 Privately Managed Portfolios

A **privately managed portfolio** is an investment account that is owned by a single investor but is overseen by a professional money manager or firm. Unlike a mutual fund, which pools money from many investors, a privately managed portfolio (also known as a **separately managed account** or SMA) contains securities that are owned directly by the individual investor. The manager has discretionary authority to buy and sell assets on the client's behalf, always acting in the client's best interest based on their specific goals, risk tolerance, and tax situation.

Risks: high minimums ($100k+); higher fees (1% - 2%); manager risk.

Upside potential: could be high, however most actively managed portfolios, including the privately managed, fail to beat the market on a consistent basis.

2.19 Algorithmic Trading

Algorithmic trading is the use of computer programs to execute trading orders based on a predefined set of instructions or rules. These algorithms analyze market data like price, time, and volume at high speeds, allowing for trades to be made and profits to be captured at a speed and frequency that a human trader cannot match.

Algorithmic trading's upside potential is notable, offering, aside from the unparalleled speed and efficiency, the elimination of emotional biases, and the ability to back test and refine strategies with precision, all while operating 24/7. It also carries significant risks, primarily due to technical failures, the potential for strategies to fail in live markets (overfitting), and the lack of human intervention in a volatile system. The core trade-off is the amplification of both risk and reward through automation.

Risks: technical failures; overfitting; lack of human oversight.

Upside potential: could be high in many cases, providing that the right technical conditions exist.

- **There is no silver bullet strategy, there are just different risk-reward relations to consider!**

Chapter 3. The Contrarian Investor

"Risk comes from not knowing what you're doing." – Warren Buffett

"The intelligent investor is a realist who sells to optimists and buys from pessimists." – Benjamin Graham

3.1 The Big Picture

A contrarian investor buys when the market is in a selling frenzy and realizes profits in a record breaking market. Despite the well-respected Efficient Market Hypothesis[21], the market isn't always right and isn't as efficient as many believe. Often, especially during strong market run-ups or drawdowns, it tends to be over-bought or oversold. This is due to human emotions and psychological factors that can lead to irrational decisions, influenced by the rapidly changing market pricing, which causes deviations from fair value. This is why timing the market is misunderstood. While the conventional financial advice is "don't try to time the market", **it's precisely those who act in a contrarian manner**

during market extremes who perform best, often beating the stock indices their portfolio stocks participate in (a feat even paid portfolio managers can rarely claim!).

3.2 Market Cycles

The global economy, far from a static entity, moves in a series of predictable, yet inherently irregular, fluctuations often referred to as cycles. These overarching economic cycles manifest more distinctly as **business cycles**, which in turn profoundly influence and interact with stock market cycles.

Business cycles, while not strictly periodic in their duration, typically comprise four distinct phases: *expansion, peak, contraction (or **recession**), and trough.* These are reflected in the Gross Domestic Product (GDP)[22], and represent the collective employment, consumer spending, business profits, capital expenditures, business investments and credit in the economy.

Stock market cycles, on the other hand, refer to the fluctuations in the prices of financial assets, particularly equities. These cycles are generally characterized by phases such as:

Accumulation: Occurs after a downturn, where astute investors begin to buy assets at what they perceive to be low prices, often when general market sentiment is still negative or neutral.

Bull Market: A period of sustained price increases, driven by growing investor confidence and increasing participation from a wider range of buyers. This phase often sees significant gains.

Distribution: As the market approaches its peak, "smart money"[23] investors begin to sell off their holdings, taking profits. Upward momentum slows, while trading volume may remain high but with less upward movement.

Bear Market: A period of declining prices, often triggered by a loss of confidence, negative news, or economic concerns. Selling accelerates, and investor sentiment becomes overwhelmingly negative. Bear markets typically occur during economic **recessions** but can also happen in other conditions.

The relationship between economic/business cycles and stock market cycles is profoundly interconnected, yet not always perfectly synchronous. The stock market is often considered a "leading indicator" of the economy because it tends to react to anticipated future conditions rather than current ones. Investors price in expectations of corporate earnings, interest rates, and overall economic health several months in advance.

However, discrepancies can arise. The stock market can overreact to news, leading to sharper swings than the underlying economic reality. It can also be influenced by factors purely related to market sentiment, speculation, or liquidity, which may not directly reflect the broader economy in the short term. For example, a "correction" in the stock market (a short-term decline) doesn't necessarily signal an impending economic recession.

Stock market negative reversals are usually categorized as follows:

Pullback: a less than a 10% decline from the recent peak in a major index. A pullback is many times merely a healthy retreat that helps in relieving pressures that were building due to overstretched valuations[24].

Correction: a decline between 10% and 20%, as investors are responding to a serious event that is perceived as having the potential to push stocks further down and into a formal bear market. A correction is over when the issue gets a relief statement or action from policy makers or when its effects appear to be short lived or transitionary. When this happens, investors tend to jump back into stocks in droves, attracted to the opportunity to buy them on the cheap.

Bear market: a drop below 20%. An economic recession is usually accompanied by a bear market in stocks. However, a bear market could arise from other reasons, such as an abrupt political crisis, a pandemic, or the popping of a sector bubble[25].

- A pullback can abruptly become a correction, which can turn into a bear market. This is due to overselling that occurs during a sentiment shock.
- A recession is a challenging event but can also be a major opportunity to boost an investment account's value.
- The model demonstrated in this guidebook is designed to flag selloff conditions for early action, likely before comforting headlines are announced and before the crowds come rushing in.

3.3 Investors' Psychological Pitfalls

"Be fearful when others are greedy, and greedy when others are fearful." – Warren Buffet

The Investor's Sentiment Cycle (and a contrarian cure!)

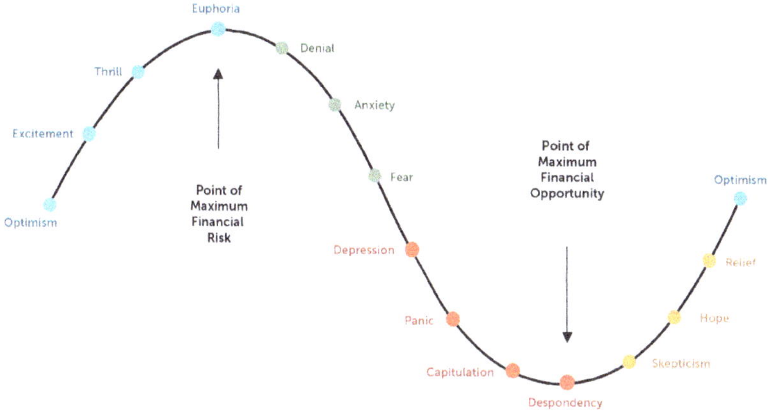

The natural urge of many stock investors is to move quickly, both into and out of a given company's stock, fast enough to ride the momentum on the way up and then exit, locking in profits before adverse headlines emerge or a market correction kicks in. This strategy is hit-or-miss unless you happen to be a company insider. Most of us retail investors are outsiders. While it might make sense when trading a single stock with little access to inside information, jumping in and out of a well-diversified portfolio, or a fund representing a large group of stocks, no longer offers a clear advantage.

Instead, a **contrarian play against the market as a whole** holds a much better potential. Here, the investor adds exposure when the market-wide selling intensifies and then proceeds to take profits when a buying frenzy takes hold, everyone rushes in, driving prices higher and setting new highs on the major indices. **This contrarian approach, if followed consistently, effectively guarantees a "buy low, sell high" result**. Aligning this with market-wide events removes idiosyncratic effects that apply to the price of individual stocks and brings into play the "put" nature of policymakers' reactions to financial market distress.

Being a successful contrarian can take significant effort and discipline to overcome a number of psychological hurdles:

Herd Mentality:

This bias describes the tendency of investors to follow the crowd, buying out of greed or selling in a panic because others are doing so. Crowds tend to overbuy and oversell, where the contrarian's goal is to take advantage of these tendencies by doing the opposite.

Recency Bias:

This bias involves giving more weight to recent events or information than to historical data. Investors might feel an urge to buy after a period of strong performance, assuming the trend will continue indefinitely. They may also be pressured to sell after a recent downturn, fearing further losses, even if the long-term prospects remain good.

- The model in this guidebook is designed to flag these events for proactive action.

Greed and Fear:

Greed in investing is characterized by an excessive desire for profit and a willingness to take on increased risk to achieve rapid gains. It often manifests as overconfidence, euphoria, and a "fear of missing out" (FOMO). Greed manifests itself in chasing returns and ignoring risk. It can fuel speculative bubbles, where asset prices become detached from their intrinsic value. Many investors, driven by greed, end up buying at market peaks, only to suffer losses when the market inevitably corrects.

Fear in investing is characterized by anxiety, panic, and a strong aversion to loss. It often arises during market downturns, economic uncertainty, or geopolitical instability. Fear leads investors to become highly risk-averse, favoring safer, lower-return assets like cash or bonds over stocks, even if stocks are trading below their intrinsic value. Fear often causes investors to sell at market lows, locking in losses and missing out on subsequent recoveries.

This **Fear & Greed Index**[26] can help in quantifying market sentiment.

FOMO (Fear of Missing Out):

Related to herd mentality and greed, it is a powerful psychological phenomenon that significantly impacts investment decisions. It describes the anxiety or apprehension an investor feels when they perceive that others are benefiting from a lucrative opportunity that they are not part of. This often leads to impulsive and irrational behavior, such as buying into assets that are rapidly increasing in price without conducting thorough due diligence or considering their own investment strategy and risk tolerance. Fueled by social media, real-time market updates, and sensationalized news, FOMO can create a herd mentality, where individuals chase trends and "hot" stocks, cryptocurrencies, or other assets purely out of fear of being left behind. This can lead to buying at market peaks and selling during corrections, ultimately undermining long-term financial goals and potentially resulting in significant losses. Understanding and actively managing FOMO is crucial for disciplined investing, encouraging investors to stick to their well-researched plans rather than being swayed by emotional impulses.

3.4 The Surprising Aspect of Long-Term Investing

We started by showing the historical exponential growth of the NASDAQ index since its inception over 50 years ago. This doesn't mean that a decades-long investment horizon is required to ensure profitability. Quite the contrary – the confidence in the inherent long-term strengths of the U.S. financial system is what draws investment capital from all over the world **at present time**, ensuring the continued growth trajectory for decades to come.

The U.S. boasts the deepest and most liquid capital markets, a dominant reserve currency, a robust regulatory framework and rule of law, an innovative and entrepreneurial culture, easy access to capital, world-renowned universities and research institutions, a very large consumer market, and the most advanced technology development industry globally.

The long term trend is our short term friend

It is for those reasons that any well-diversified investment in the U.S. stock market, particularly in the technology sector, should become profitable within a reasonable amount of time, and very profitable thereafter. This could result in frequent opportunities for taking profits (we'll call this **"residual income"** in the context of this model). It is, in fact, what the model simulation later in the book demonstrates. **This is a benefit that a well-designed long-term strategy will provide in the short and medium term!**

All this holds true provided a strategy such as the one presented in this guidebook is deployed **consistently**!

3.5 The Strategy

The strategy in this guidebook follows a set of buy and sell rules that collectively signal entry and exit points. These rules are designed to align with extreme conditions of market lows (for buying) and new cycle highs (for selling).

The strategy has the following characteristics:

- Growth-oriented
- Moderately aggressive
- Well diversified
- Actively trades at market highs and lows
- Investor time requirement for daily tracking is 15 to 30 minutes typically - with occasional trading included (more trading is expected during market extremes).

A practical example (case study) for such a strategy is given in a later chapter. The exercise covers a recent six-year period where extremes in market highs and lows were repeated several times. Despite the frequent turbulence, the portfolio achieved a **three-fold appreciation** (in nominal terms), handily beating all major indices.

Chapter 4. Unveiling the Model: A Deep Dive

4.1 The Big Picture – a Chart That Says It All

NASDAQ Since Inception

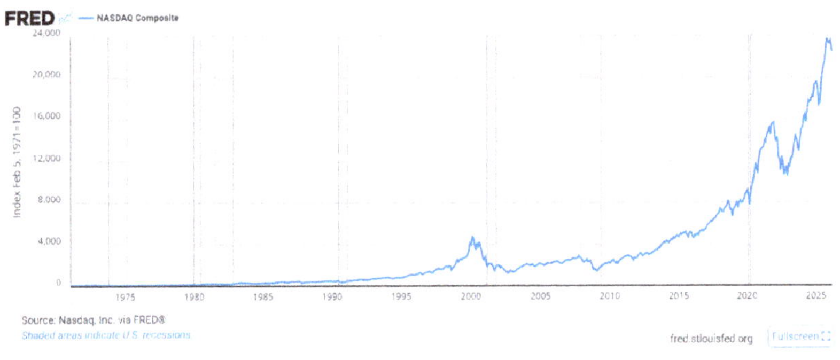

(Shaded areas indicate U.S. recessions)

Key events in NASDAQ history:

1971: NASDAQ founded

1987: Black Monday crash

2000: Dot-com bubble peak

2001: Dot-com crash

2008: Financial crisis

2020: Covid recovery

2022: Tech sell-off

From looking at the chart above it is quite clear that the aggregate performance of the publicly traded stocks that contribute to the index has grown exponentially since its inception. This applies to other major indices as well, such as the S&P 500 and the Dow Jones Industrial Average. It reflects a fundamental nature of U.S. and global economic growth and should continue in the future, albeit over long periods of time. As mentioned before, it is driven by economic, political and behavioral reasons. This, among other factors, is also what drives the **time value of money**[27], or the benefit of putting money to work early. It is, however, also quite easy to observe that there are periods where, after reaching a certain peak, the index falls significantly and continues to drift lower for quite some time before resuming its accelerated increase in price. Both the drop and the increase reflect the expected performance of businesses as a result of market-moving events (such as the 1970s oil embargo, the 2008 financial crisis or the COVID pandemic), or a policy action by the Federal Reserve, the Congress or the administration. If the aggregate interpretation of the investor community is that businesses' profits will grow, they will buy the stocks of these businesses at higher prices and the index will rise. Conversely, an expected decline in profits will result in stocks being sold at lower prices, causing the index to fall. **For a contrarian investor, a falling stock market is an opportunity to get in and buy, as a resumption of the exponential growth is expected on the other side of the current event.**

Recent analyses of historical U.S. stock market data, such as those conducted on the S&P 500 and Dow Jones indices, generally support the claim that bull markets—periods when prices are rising—tend to last significantly longer than bear markets. Though exact proportions can vary depending on the timeframe and methodology used, it is commonly cited that the market is in a bull phase roughly two-thirds of the time, while bear markets take up about one-third or less. This reflects the long-term upward trajectory of major equity indices, with downturns being shorter but sometimes sharper.

- Note: although price fluctuations in the more recent years (right side of the chart) seem much larger than in the earlier years (left side), they aren't truly so, as the real magnitude of each change is relative to the scale at the time. For instance, the 1987 "Black Monday" crash that looks like a minor blip on the chart, has actually erased roughly a third of the index, a severe event by all accounts!

4.2 Trendlines and How They Support Investment Decisions

A trendline in our case is a best-fit calculation that serves as a prediction for the next set of data points in a graph. Since the stock market indices above appear to grow exponentially, we'll use the **exponential fit** trendline in Excel as depicted below:

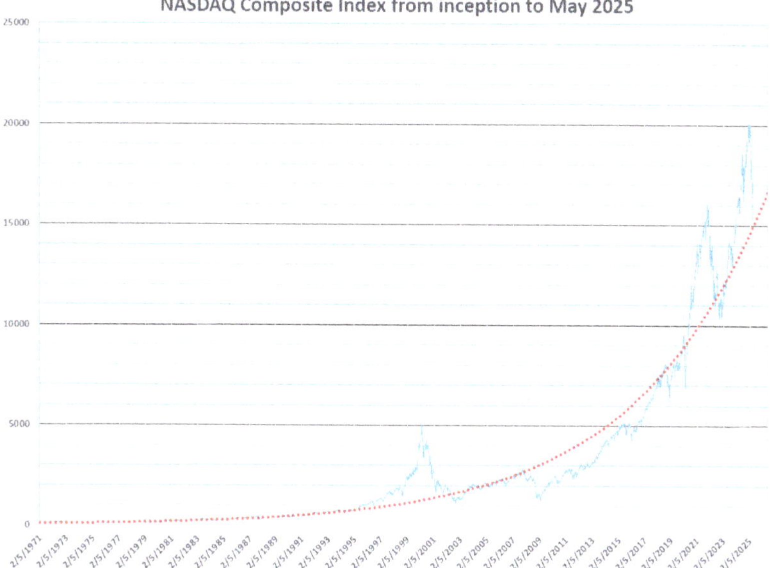

The trendline here (in Red) is calculated from the historical price points since the NASDAQ Composite Index's inception in 1971 up until May 2025.

The trendline splits the index line chart into two regions: price points above the trendline, and price points below. **This presents the first strategy of our model: when the index drops below the trendline, more accumulation of stock positions should take place than when it's above the trendline. Similarly, when above the trendline, more rebalancing and profit taking should be done than when below it.** At any given time, the farther away the current price is from the trendline level, the more aggressive the buying (when below) or profit taking (when above) should be.

How is this trendline different from a moving average indicator?

Moving average indicators are used frequently in technical analysis[28], a system that helps in making trading decisions based on chart patterns. Moving averages are calculated based on recent price data, usually up to 200 days. In a downward trend, a moving average indicator will usually be crossed well before the historical long term trendline, perhaps multiple times, thereby providing a short-term signal without the historical context. While moving averages can serve us well in uptrend corrections, for the purpose of the model discussed here, the trendline remains the ultimate reference level for how close a bear market is to a turnaround.

- Note that it can be argued that going back 50 years may skew the results, as economic environments keep changing quite significantly over the years. This is a valid point; however, the overall pattern should be relevant to future events even if triggers are different. Regardless, it is still up to the individual investor to decide what period to use for building the trendline.
- Note also that the trendline function is accurate for the moment in time it is being calculated. Different times in the past may have gotten somewhat different trendlines, being shifted up or down relative to the stock index line chart. This is because the trendline is calculated based on historical data points up to that moment. The investment rule above should still hold, as the trendline is just a best estimate for where the index is trending in future months and years given the information at hand.
- Go to Appendix C.2 to learn more about setting up trendlines in Excel.

4.3 Why Sell?

The logic for why to buy when stock prices turn cheap is fairly straightforward. But in an exponentially growing stock market valuation over the long run, why is it a good idea to sell periodically into new highs? Why not let the portfolio grow without interruption?

The justification for selling is based on a presumed need for budget management. When the stock market drops sharply, other assets should be liquidated and used to acquire more exposure to stocks. The assumption is that these resources are limited and should be replenished when there's an opportunity to do so.

In addition, a disciplined investor would keep in mind the target balance between stocks and other assets (e.g. 60/40 for stocks to fixed income) in their portfolio and would try to rebalance when possible. Taking profits is also preferred by investors who feel that stocks are overbought, and valuations are stretched, which, in a contrarian context, are predictors of an upcoming correction.

Moreover, when investments are used to complement retirement income or to fund other needs, it may be better to sell preemptively at the top rather than risk being forced to do so in a down market.

- Selling at a top is beneficial just as much as adding at a bottom. Both are healthy ways to prevent greed and fear from slowing down or reversing portfolio growth!

Chapter 5. The Model in Action

"D"on't look for the needle, buy the haystack". – John Bogle

5.1 The Big Picture

A cross below the historical trendline[29] acts as a strong technical signal indicating that the stock market is cheap and warrants involvement, as the likelihood of long-term gains is higher than normal. However, this event does not happen very often. In fact, it has occurred only a handful of times in the last decade. While it is entirely possible to keep a stack of cash on the sideline in an interest-bearing savings account or a Money Market fund, all the while waiting for this rare downward crossing to happen, a prudent investor may find that other valid opportunities to play the market in a risk-managed manner do exist. This chapter will cover a trading model that supports this approach while generating income for the investor from the profits.

Buy low, sell high is the most common approach to profit from trading stocks (there are trades that reverse the order by 'selling short' – these will not be playing a part in our model). However, buying low and selling high is easier said than done. Traders find it quite difficult to identify truly low entry points. In fact, many times they end up buying high and selling lower out of fear of losing their invested principal when their particular stock or the entire market sinks.

5.2 Trade Indicators

There are quite a few indicators that can help identify buying opportunities. The model here uses indicators that apply to broad market indices (as opposed to indicators of individual stocks). This is because when a major index makes a strong move downwards, it often pulls down many otherwise healthy stocks and sectors with it. It is therefore easier to find opportunities in individual stocks or in ETFs during periods of overall stock market weakness. Similarly, a market at record highs points to profit-taking opportunities across many of the underlying stocks and ETFs.

The model's daily buy & sell indicators

Our tools employ an **AI-powered algorithm** to process market data and to set the levels of the following indicators (and others), which in turn will collectively trigger buy and sell trade alerts:

The NASDAQ historical trendline: where is the index relative to it today? Under or over will contribute to a buy or sell decision respectively, and so will the proximity to the line from below or from above.

The VIX (Volatility Index)[30]: is it above the model's threshold today?

Daily change: is the index up or down today and by how much?

Relative drop: by how much has the index dropped since the last record high?

Record high: is the index breaking new highs today? This could influence a decision to sell.

Profit margin: is the account profitable today and by how much? This could influence a sell decision.

Buy and sell amounts determination

Buy amount: The model uses a percentage of today's ETF portfolio value.

Sell amount: The model uses a percentage of the trading day's dollar value appreciation.

5.3 Why ETFs?

The asset class this guide prefers to start with is stock-based ETFs[31]. They're a good match for the need for **liquidity, flexibility, low-cost trading and built-in diversification**.

ETFs are traded intraday like stocks and are easy to buy and sell instantly. ETFs contain multiple stocks that usually belong to the same sector, industry or theme. When building a contrarian trading model, picking promising sectors over individual stocks has strategic importance: it allows us to ride new trends in technology, business and policy without dealing with unique situations and risk profiles of individual companies. With that, ETFs enable the technical and fundamental analysis decisions to be applied efficiently to a basket of similar stocks as a group.

Moreover, selecting these ETFs by their correlation with the technology sector allows the model to use market-level thresholds to signal trade opportunities. Specifically, our model uses these features along with a careful selection of ETFs that are highly correlated with the NASDAQ Composite Index. This enhances the potential of our contrarian strategy to maximize its performance.

- **The model seeks to diversify within the technology sector to minimize specific (unsystematic) risk, while maintaining a high correlation with the NASDAQ in a contrarian way for maximizing growth potential.**

Finally, with their built-in, professionally-managed diversification, the leading high quality stocks in each industry are assigned their appropriate **weights** by the fund itself – a significant benefit to the investor.

- Ideally, a **hybrid portfolio** consisting of sector ETFs as well as a selection of individual stocks could work well for our purpose. However, building and managing such a portfolio would be too complex for a start. Therefore, for the purpose of gaining experience with the concepts in this guide, a portfolio comprised purely of ETFs would be a safer choice.
- Help with complementing the model with a selection of individual stocks is coming soon to the website[32].

5.4 Selecting the Portfolio Holdings

- The ETF list below, to this day, is effective in fulfilling the goals of the strategy laid out in this guide. However, it's possible that other ETFs could be used based on the specific circumstances and how well they correlate with the NASDAQ Composite Index. A list of such optional ETFs has been added to this chapter. Updates on this topic, as well as changes in the relative weights will be published on the website.

The first ETF choice is the Invesco QQQ Trust (**QQQ**)[33] (Large-cap-growth, 102 stocks) which tracks the NASDAQ-100 index[34], representing some of the largest-cap[35] stocks in the NASDAQ Composite Index. Its weight in our model portfolio: 35%.

The next ETF choice is The Technology Select Sector SPDR Fund (**XLK**)[36] (Large-cap-growth, 71 stocks), which tracks the Technology Select Sector Index. Weight in the model portfolio: 35%

- QQQ and XLK represent generally more growth-oriented stocks, which normally would make them appreciate faster in a rising market. These ETFs, however, are also quite volatile, as growth stocks[37] often get hit harder in a market correction. They would also typically have a **stronger recovery** coming out of the correction, which makes them a good fit for our concept.

Other ETFs that could be considered for added diversification:

The SPDR S&P 500 ETF (**SPY**)[38] (Large-Cap blend, 504 stocks) tracks the S&P 500[39] index and is a good choice for tracking a market-wide selection of stocks. The S&P 500 index, together with the Dow Jones Industrial Average and the NASDAQ Composite Index, are widely viewed as representing the state of the overall U.S. stock market. Model weight: 20%.

The iShares Russel 2000 ETF (**IWM**)[40] (Small-cap blend, 1,982 stocks) tracks the Russell 2000[41] small-cap index. Small-cap stocks usually break out in the accelerating phase of the economic cycle during which they could outperform the other indices. They may, however, lag behind at other times but should still be included albeit at a smaller share. Model weight: 10%

Going down the ladder from the market-wide ETFs, **sector-based ETFs** target narrower markets with growth potential. An optional list is provided later in this chapter.

5.5 The Top-Down Approach

In this approach, the decision to buy or sell a security is **based on its predetermined exposure** within the portfolio. Instead of making trading decisions for each security separately, a **trading trigger** is applied to the portfolio as a whole and is then distributed down to its constituents based on a **relative exposure weight** that is preassigned to each position.

This approach significantly simplifies the **timing of trades** and **risk calculations** for the individual ETF positions. Since with this model trade triggers are based on **market-wide events** and **portfolio-level value/performance criteria**, the required trades for the individual ETFs can be derived and executed quickly and efficiently. The trading strategy is consistent and balanced, and the entire process can be easily automated, if desired.

Example:

A portfolio consists of 3 ETFs: A, B & C. Each is assigned a weight based on its expected performance and risk profile. Weights in this example are A=40%, B=35%, C=25%.

Now assume market conditions have met certain thresholds and a trade alert was triggered, and that a trade amount of **$2,000** is calculated based on the portfolio size. This portfolio-level amount is then broken down to each position according to its pre-assigned weight:

- A will be traded with $800 (40% of $2,000)
- B with $700 (35% of $2,000)

- C with $500 (25% of $2,000)

The exposure weight is assigned based on the security's **upside potential** and its overall **risk profile**. When this assessment changes, new relative weights are assigned for quick action when market conditions are ripe.

This method can be applied to a group of securities that follow a common **leading index** with a **high historical correlation**. For our model, the chosen leading index is the **NASDAQ Composite** for the reasons discussed next.

5.6 Why Choose a Technology Sector Concentration?

It's not hard to notice that technology stocks make up the largest portion of our ETF model portfolio. This is largely because technology is the **strongest cyclical growth sector**. Its significant growth potential, high margins and mass-market reach attract capital from across the globe. Furthermore, it's a primary driver for **productivity**[42] improvements in the U.S. economy.

Technology stocks demonstrate rapid growth due to their inherent **innovative nature** and **disruptive potential**, making them a powerful growth engine for the global economy and for the sector itself. Recent examples include the internet and e-commerce revolution, mobile computing and smartphones, cloud computing, and more recently, artificial intelligence (AI), machine learning and robotics. AI, in particular, is widely considered the next major technological revolution, followed by cloud computing, cybersecurity, autonomous systems and space exploration.

Given the immense capital allocations, both from private and public (government) sources into these areas, it is widely believed that the technology sector will experience **explosive growth** in the next decade and beyond,

It's crucial to remember that being cyclical, the technology sector could also suffer more than others during economic slowdowns. **These wide swings from high growth to deep lows and vice versa (!) is precisely what enhances the investing concept in this guide, potentially leading to stronger performance relative to the index.**

- **Sector rotation is not recommended**: there is evidence that some sectors perform better than others in different stages of the economic cycle. Attempting to time this, in the author's view, complicates the model by introducing too many variables. Sticking with the technology sector throughout the cycle offers a more consistent and focused approach (as long as the investor can stomach the large swings!).

- **Does the ETF selection ever change?** Yes, it does. Over time, new sectors may take the lead in the technology frontier, and others may get pushed back or become obsolete altogether. It is therefore advised to stay current on technological trends. However, it is **not** recommended to jump the gun and put money on the line assuming that any single emerging technology that happens to capture headlines today will ultimately become economically viable down the road.

- The **top-down approach** described earlier, i.e. **following a major index and its volatility indicators to identify trading opportunities in a portfolio of weighted ETF positions**, can work not just with the NASDAQ but also with the S&P 500, the Dow Jones, the Russel 2000 or other major indices. That is, as long as the selected ETFs have a **high historical correlation** with the chosen leading index.

5.7 Optional ETFs

Below is a list of additional ETFs that should work well with our model. They represent the industries discussed above, all of which are highly correlated with the NASDAQ Composite Index.

Having different growth industries in the mix provides an additional lever to pull when expecting relative strength in one or another.

You may choose from the list below to add or replace an existing ETF position:

SMH[43]: composed mainly of stocks in the semiconductor industry (large-cap-growth). Model weight: 20%.

HACK[44]: composed mainly of stocks of companies that provide cybersecurity technology and services (mid-cap-growth). Model weight: 20%.

WCLD[45]: tracks cloud computing software and services (small-cap-growth). Model weight: 10%.

UFO[46]: space-related businesses such as satellite technology (small-cap-blend). Model weight: 10%.

ITA[47]: aerospace and defense sector (large-cap-growth). Model weight: 10%.

IGV[48]: software industry (large-cap-growth). Model weight: 20%.

ARKQ[49]: autonomous technology and robotics (mid-cap-growth). Model weight: 20%.

ARTY[50]: artificial intelligence technologies (large-cap-growth). Model weight: 20%

- Weights must sum up to 100%.
- Model weights are subject to change. The most up-to-date weights are found on the app.

5.8 Finding Bottom

The term "**finding the bottom**" refers to the act of identifying and buying an asset at its lowest possible price point before its value begins to recover and rise. It represents the ultimate ideal of "buying low" to maximize profit and is the most rewarded trade if executed successfully.

While a successful trading strategy that catches the bottom will also likely identify nearby price points for buying opportunities - making the lowest price less crucial in the long run - finding the absolute bottom is still considered a strong indication of an effective trading strategy. As the charts below demonstrate, our simulation model has successfully found bottom in all three market cycles!

5.9 Is This Just Another Algo?

In some respects, there are similarities to algorithmic trading platforms, or 'algos'. Much like algos, our model analyzes market conditions and applies a set of rules to initiate trades.

There are some stark differences, though:

While traditional algos focus mainly on short-term strategies that are applied to individual stocks, our model offers a **long-term, top-down** (portfolio-level) view, based on a proven system built around ETF investing.

Moreover, algos perform best by automating trades while skipping the investor's input. In their system, timing and speed - often down to the very second - are crucial. This leaves no time for investor involvement. In contrast, our model empowers investors to execute less time-critical, **carefully guided trades** on their own, thereby helping them build confidence and resist biases that can limit performance. In our system, performance is measured in months, not seconds, and is long-lived by design.

Finally, while algos rely on identifying intermittent conditions that create temporary trading opportunities, our model leverages the inherent dynamics of the U.S. economy and its long-term **exponential growth**, with the aim of building long-lasting wealth.

Chapter 6. A Case Study

Below is a simulated performance analysis for a new portfolio, starting in 2019 and managed throughout the COVID pandemic crash, the 2021 bounce, the 2022 downturn, the 2023-2024 bull market and the recent tariffs-induced correction and subsequent recovery, encompassing **three cycles of strong lows and highs with varying durations**.

The exercise simulates transactions based on the portfolio positions and trading rules laid out in previous chapters. Performance is evaluated at the end of the period.

The data set used for measuring and comparing performance consists of **real historical daily market closing prices**.

6.1 Direct Comparison to Major Indices

- Time period: from May 23, 2019, to May 22, 2025
- Portfolio ETFs weights: QQQ 35%, XLK 35%, SPY 20%, IWM 10%
- *Model performance against indices for the full period:*

NASDAQ +148.1%

S&P 500 +107.0%

Dow Jones +64.2%

Model Portfolio +197.2%

• *Performance as measured at the market's low points:*

May 23, 2019 to Mar 23, 2020:

NASDAQ: -10.0% S&P 500: -20.7% **Model: -12.9%**

May 23, 2019 to October 12, 2022:

NASDAQ: +36.6% S&P 500: +26.7% **Model: +64.7%**

May 23, 2019 to April 8, 2025:

NASDAQ: +100.2% S&P 500: +88.8% **Model: +134.2%**

6.2 The Charts

- **The reacceleration effect**: note how, for short periods in 2021, the model lagged somewhat behind but then regained powerful momentum from mid-2022 onward. This was the effect of profit-taking during the strong market of late 2021. This paid off later when the realized funds were reused to build up the next profit cycle.

- **Taking profits serves multiple purposes**: it recharges the investor's cash reserves (or the 40% in a 60/40 split port-folio) that would be used later to buy into a cheaply priced market when the cycle turns. It also reduces exposure to an inevitable bear market, such as the one that started in No-vember 2021. Finally, in an extended bull market run, it has the potential to provide extra income in the form of cash flow.

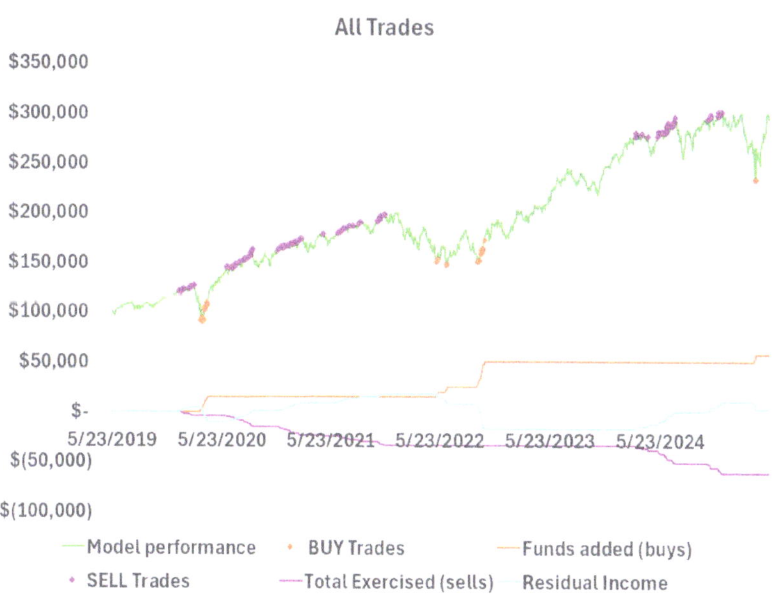

- Buy and sell trades are based on trade alerts generated by the model's web app.
- The full Excel simulation is available for download from the website[51].

6.3 Model Performance Summary

- **Initial allocation:**

$100,000 into ETFs
$50,000 into cash (sweep account)

- **Total value at period end:**

$294,461 in ETFs
$52,784 in cash

- **Annualized ROR (Rate of Return):**

+20.29%

- **Added profit vs. organic growth (no trades):**

$34,631 (19.25%)

- **Buy transactions:**

26

- **Buy transaction total:**

$57,836 in total

- **Sell transactions**:

108

- **Sell transaction total:**

$60,620 in total

- **Largest draw from the reserves:**

$17,255

6.4 Comparing to Pro-Managed Plans

Model ROR +20.29%

Top 5 actively managed funds, 5 year annualized return

1, Fidelity Select Technology Portfolio +18.76%

2. Loomis Sayles Growth Fund (Class Y) +17.66%

3. Vanguard Global Capital Cycles Fund +16.78%

4. T. Rowe Price All-Cap Opportunities Fund +16.18%

5. AAM Brentview Dividend Growth ETF +15.98%

As of Jul/Aug 2025 (Source: Google Gemini 2.5 Pro)

6.5 Staying Invested (Very Important!)

When putting money in a long-term **savings account**, the common practice is to leave it there to grow via compounding interest over time. When it comes to the **stock market**, investments can grow much faster but can also drop just as fast, which can become uncomfortable to watch, to say the least. The purpose of this book is to show that **investing patiently**, all the while acting in a **contrarian fashion**, can be extremely rewarding when your savings are eventually used to fund life's big expenditures. This approach to **saving by investing** can offer a much higher compounding effect than a conventional savings account.

Please continue reading and find out more about the **rationale** behind this thinking and the **steps** to take to put this savings strategy into practice.

Chapter 7. The Informed Trader: A Fundamental View

"The stock market is a device for transferring money from the impatient to the patient." – Warren Buffett
"Don't fight the Fed." – Market Wisdom

7.1 The Economy and the Stock Market: What's Important?

While the stock market often acts as a barometer for economic sentiment, it's vital to recognize its distinct characteristics and forward-looking nature. The economy provides the fundamental backdrop of corporate performance, but market dynamics, investor psychology, and a host of other factors shape stock valuations. For effective decision-making, it's important to analyze both sets of indicators, understanding that while they frequently move in tandem, their individual complexities and lead-lag relationships require careful and nuanced interpretation.

At its core, the economy reflects the aggregate production, distribution, and consumption of goods and services within a nation. Key economic indicators like **Gross Domestic Product (GDP)**, **employment rates**, **inflation** (measured by the **Consumer Price Index** or **Producer Price Index**), **retail sales**, and **industrial production** offer insights into the overall health and direction of economic activity. A growing GDP signifies increased output and a stronger economy, which typically translates to higher corporate earnings and consumer spending. Low unemployment indicates a robust labor market, leading to greater disposable income and sustained consumption. Conversely, high inflation can erode purchasing power and business profitability, while rising unemployment signals economic contraction.

The stock market, on the other hand, is a forward-looking mechanism. Stock prices are largely driven by investor expectations about future corporate earnings and the broader economic outlook. This anticipatory nature means the market often "leads" the economy, reacting to perceived future changes rather than merely reflecting present conditions. For instance, a stock market rally might begin even before an economic recovery is fully evident, as investors discount future growth prospects. Similarly, a market downturn can precede a recession, reflecting collective fears about upcoming economic challenges.

Several critical factors influence both the economy and the stock market. **Monetary policy**, set by central banks through **interest rates**, is paramount. Lower interest rates typically encourage borrowing and investment, stimulating economic growth and making stocks more attractive relative to bonds. **Fiscal policy**, encompassing government spending and taxation, also plays a significant role. Political stability, global trade relations, technological advancements, and even unforeseen events like natural disasters or pandemics can exert profound influence. For individual stocks, company-specific news, earnings reports, management changes, and industry trends are equally important.

Despite their close ties, the stock market and the real economy can diverge for several reasons. The stock market is heavily influenced by market sentiment, which can be prone to irrational exuberance or panic, leading to bubbles or crashes that don't always align with underlying economic fundamentals. Furthermore, the benefits of a rising stock market are not evenly distributed across the population. A significant portion of stock ownership is concentrated among the wealthiest households, meaning stock market performance might not directly reflect the financial well-being of the average citizen, whose income primarily comes from wages.

7.2 Economic Releases: What to Follow?

Economic releases, often tracked through an **economic calendar**, are scheduled announcements of economic data and events that offer insights into the health and performance of a country's or region's economy. These releases are critical because they can significantly impact financial markets, including stocks, bonds, and foreign exchange rates.

Releases with a HIGH stock market impact:

- FOMC (Federal Open Market Committee) Interest Rate Decision
- Labor market: Unemployment Claims; Unemployment Rate; Nonfarm Payrolls; Average Hourly Earnings; Average Workweek
- Personal income; Personal Spending; PCE Prices

- Inflation: CPI (Consumer Price Index); PPI (Producer Price Index)
- Retail Sales
- Housing market: Housing Starts; Building Permits; New Home Sales; Existing Home Sales
- Crude Oil Inventories
- Purchasing Managers Index: U.S. Manufacturing PMI; U.S. Services PMI
- ISM Manufacturing Index; ISM Services Index
- Consumer Confidence
- The "high impact" label needs to be taken in the context of a largely stable system. No single economic release would typically cause mayhem, as all are subject to some month-to-month "noise". A release that diverges strongly from expectations may result in some stock market movement but would usually only start a serious decline or a strong increase if it aligns with other indicators, both technical and economic, adding to an already generally negative or positive sentiment, respectively.
- Aggregate company earnings forecasts, such as the **S&P 500 Earnings and Estimate Report,** can also move markets if a strong trend, negative or positive, is noticed.
- Prominent sources for economic releases and commentary:

Trading Economics[52]
Investing.com[53]
Briefing.com[54]

7.3 Does the State of the Economy Even Matter?

It's the inherent nature of the U.S. economy and by extension the stock market to grow exponentially over the long run. This trend is driven by growth in GDP and corporate earnings, increased efficiency and productivity, new industries and disruptive technologies, as well as expanding globalization. This exponential growth is also occasionally interrupted due to several possible factors, including inflation and policy over-correction, financial imbalances and valuation bubbles[55], supply shocks, pandemics, and so on, causing slowdowns or full scale recessions. All of these, with varying magnitudes, are generally repeating patterns that can be expected to continue.

Our model leverages all of the above by selecting to focus on a strong growth sector category, while recharging at times of extreme weakness and beating the index during the extended expansion periods that follow.

Given this predictive profile, are the economic releases and other market information necessary to follow, or is it enough to only act upon quantitatively generated trade alerts?

This is a choice that's up to the individual investor to make. Being attached to financial news and analysis can work in different ways. On one hand, for some, it may induce over-reaction, especially when panic takes over Wall Street. It's not easy to overcome the natural tendency to follow the herd. On the other hand, personally, I prefer to be informed and educated as it builds an understanding of the cross-currents that affect financial markets, which in turn helps with expectations, builds confidence and adds to the experience.

Chapter 8. Get Started with Your Own ETF Portfolio

"You haven't lost until you sell at a loss" – Warren Buffett
"The most important thing about an investment philosophy is that you have one you can stick with." – David Booth

- Some sections in this chapter assume you are embarking on your investment journey for the first time. If you already have a stock portfolio in place, then please skip as seems appropriate.

8.1 Step 1: Open a Trading Account

To begin using this investing model you will need to **fund a brokerage account** that is approved for trading stocks. This can be either a retirement account (tax deferred) or a taxable account.

Any amount, big or small, can be used with this model, assuming your brokerage firm[56]:

1. Does not charge a fee for stock transactions (brokerages nowadays typically don't charge).

2. **Allows to specify trade orders in dollar amounts** or fractional shares (rather than in whole shares) for **any security**. This is preferred to avoid being forced to trade in amounts that do not align with the model's calculations.

401(k), 403(b) Considerations

Access to exchange-traded funds (ETFs) in a 401(k) depends on the specific plan offered by your employer. While ETFs are becoming more common, most 401(k) plans traditionally offer a limited menu of mutual funds and collective investment trusts. If this is your case, **it is all right to use mutual funds instead, as long as you can trade them directly**. For the purpose of this model, it is preferred to pick funds that are closely associated with the technology sector.

Here's how you might be able to invest in ETFs within your 401(k):

Method 1: Through a core investment menu

Some forward-thinking employers are adding ETFs directly to their plan's main investment lineup, particularly in the form of ETF-based target-date funds. However, this is still not the norm, and mutual funds remain the dominant option in most plans.

Method 2: Using a Self-Directed Brokerage Account (SDBA)

A more common route is an SDBA, which acts like a mini brokerage account within your 401(k). If your employer offers this option:

- You can gain access to a much wider variety of investment choices, including virtually any ETF.
- You are responsible for making your own trades, rather than relying on the plan's default options.

- Some plans may limit the portion of your account balance you can allocate to the SDBA.

To find out if you can trade ETFs, check your Summary Plan Description or log into your plan provider's website. If an SDBA is available, you will likely need to opt-in and move money from your core fund options into that account.

8.2 Step 2: Set Up a Budgetary Cash Reserve

Before making our first purchases, the model requires us to decide on the portion of the budget allocated to the **cash reserve**.

The cash reserve, in the context of this model, is the portion not allocated to ETFs. For example, if we choose a traditional 60/40 ratio of stocks to bonds, the 40% will serve as our cash reserve, to be used opportunistically during times of stock market extreme weakness to buy into the low priced market. Any **cash-equivalent asset**[57] can be used here.

Alternatively, the percentage share in cash can also be based on the index's position relative to the **historical trendline**[58]. Below are possible **initial allocations** for the NASDAQ index (based mostly on historical precedence). These allocations will apply when creating a new portfolio or when adding new funds to the budget. After setting this starting point, cash management will be done dynamically based on market conditions and portfolio appreciation.

- Index is lower than 10% below the trendline: keep a minimum of 10% in cash.
- 10% below to 10% above the trendline: keep a minimum of 20% in cash.

- 10% to 30% above the trendline: keep a minimum of 30% in cash.
- 30% or more above the trendline: keep a minimum of 40% in cash.

The reason for the growing cash reserves is to provide a cushion against a possible strong market turn-around. As a bull market extends higher, more pressure builds on the market's "smart money" participants to take profits, out of fear of a sudden reversal. This reversal can be the result of a policy move from the Federal Reserve, or the Congress, or the administration, a geopolitical crisis, or internal imbalances that are building in the economy when growth goes wild. When these occur at market highs, the drop can be severe as investors rush out in an attempt to protect their investments.

- Note that investors may set their own reserve levels. Investors may also choose a different technical indicator, such as the "200-day moving average", in place of the historical trendline this model is using. This is acceptable as long as they feel prepared for a lengthy bear market with enough cash on hand to take advantage of the resulting dip in stock prices.
- **Reserves do not simply sit around**. Traditionally, they are supposed to be invested in bonds, but they can also be put into cash-equivalent assets, those which are interest-bearing short-term instruments, such as Money Market funds. Some brokerages provide **sweep accounts** that pay interest and execute the cash transfers seamlessly in alignment with stock trading transactions.

8.3 Step 3: Fund the Selected Portfolio Positions

The ETF selections[59] above represent some of the best-performing sectors with the highest future potential at the time of writing this guidebook. The onset of AI technology is rapidly gaining speed and pulling many other sectors along for the ride.

Hence, for the initial funding allocations, we'll start by giving the technology-heavy ETFs more weight:

QQQ: 35%

XLK: 35%

SPY: 20%

IWM: 10%

Including other ETFs[60] is possible as long as the total weights add up to 100%.

Funding is done directly with your brokerage. Your trades need to be updated into the model's tool you're using in order to receive timely trade alerts.

8.4 How to Get started With Monthly Contributions

To get on with the model using monthly installments, you may start by allocating the portions that will go into the stock market and towards fixed income, for example, a 60%/40% split between ETFs and Money Market. Then proceed with monthly investing using this same split while updating the model's tool accordingly. When a "buy" trade alert is generated, you may cash out the calculated amount from the cash-equivalent reserve portion and buy ETFs with it in your brokerage account. This method is similar to Dollar-Cost Averaging[61], albeit with a more active role for the investor.

8.5 Step 4: Set Up the Model's Trade-Alerts Engine

- The model can be built in Excel or even using a hand calculator. However for automating the daily tracking and for generating trade alerts the app is the better option. If you choose to go with the manual process, Appendix C describes it in detail.

The model's tools (included in the web app) generate trade alerts based on market and portfolio conditions. You will input your portfolio positions and their relative weights, and the app will calculate buy or sell amounts for the portfolio when the set conditions trigger an alert. The model's top ETF picks and weights are displayed for reference.

Trade alerts are generated based on market and portfolio measures meeting certain thresholds in real-time (i.e., during trading hours). After generating a trade alert, the model will then calculate the **portfolio-level** total amount to buy or sell and break this total down to **individual trade amounts** for each ETF position based on their assigned allocations (weights). Thresholds get AI-defined defaults that can be customized for setting a personalized strategy.

8.6 Step 5: Track the Action

The app will track and display the movements in your portfolio positions and the indices relevant to the model. To track the general markets you may refer to publicly available online financial tools, such as Yahoo Finance.

In most trading days, major indices normally move up or down by less than 1%. Special attention should be given to larger moves, as they would point to possible extended runs to the downside or the upside, presenting buy or sell opportunities respectively. When the conditions specified in the model match your portfolio's state, the engine will generate a personal trade alert along with the amounts to buy or sell. When an alert is issued, it is advised to act on it in a timely manner as market conditions could change quickly.

It is important to remember that **the model's trade alerts are contrarian in nature**, which means that sell alerts will likely come in just when the market is running strong and FOMO[62] pressure is high! Similarly, buy alerts are given when the market is selling off, and herd behavior is in full swing!

Additionally, since over time the market trends up more often than down, it is statistically more likely that several sell alerts will come before the first buy alert!

- Typically, a single trade alert is issued in a trading day when the conditions are met. Additional intraday alerts may occur in the rare cases of exceptionally large moves in the index.
- Daily time commitment: when alerted, it should take no more than 15-30 minutes to place the trades and to update back the model with the modified positions. Trade alerts are expected in about 10% of all trading days under our current model.
- It is prudent to check economic and financial market news on most days, even in mild action days when no trade alerts are expected.
- The model, by design, generates "buy" alerts in conditions of extreme market stress, or a "bear market", which do not occur regularly. In an extreme event, there are usually multiple consecutive days when "buy" alerts will be issued. Sometimes the situation reemerges shortly after the first alert, but

it's also possible that the next extreme condition may only occur months down the road. Thus, it's important to act on "buy" signals in a timely manner to maximize profits later on. It is also important not to get caught in the day-to-day fluctuations, however strong they may be, but to wait instead for the true, long-term opportunities. There will be more days with a "sell" signal than with a "buy", and many days where you'll remain passive, just watching the action.

- The reason "sell" alerts are typically more common than "buy" alerts is that the market tends to be in an upswing longer than otherwise. However, if you've just started, note that the engine will wait for some profits to build up before alerting you for cashing some of them out. This is done to allow the portfolio value to build upon its growth potential.

- It is important to remember that frequent market fluctuations are normal and are not by themselves a reason to feel pressure to act outside of the model.

- The model was back-tested with real historical market prices. However, it is important to note that it may not be perfect in all possible real-life scenarios that may arise (e.g., it may not "catch" the exact day the cycle bottoms every single time). There are **no perfect models** out there, hence all that can be done is to try to follow rules that have a **better chance** of finding the optimal "buy low, sell high" conditions.

8.7 Adding to the Positions

A strong market drop is the time to consider putting some of the reserves to work. At this point a decision is needed as to which position to add and by how much. Here we may want to add to the historically stronger positions (those that grew their portfolio share relative to the others), or the ones believed to have a strong recovery potential or simply split them according to some ratio.

The engine will propose the dollar amount to put towards the new purchase for each ETF based on its default weight or user-assigned weights. The user has a few considerations when assigning weights. Say that our portfolio has 2 ETFs, QQQ with a 45% share and XLK with 55%, and the original split when purchased was 50/50. We could choose between the following 3 options:

1. Go 50/50. This will help rebalance the portfolio back towards the original split.
2. Stay with the current balance of 45/55. This will recognize the relative strength of XLK.
3. Decide on a new split based on expectations for future performance and downside risk.

- The web-based model will occasionally update the default split based on its internal algorithm's predictions.
- A market-wide drop, as reflected in the NASDAQ index, will be the main trigger for a buy decision. Since our top picks portfolio is well-diversified within the technology sector, it will mostly follow the NASDAQ index on the way down as well as on the way back up. Depending on portfolio composition, it may move more or less than the index in either direction, but it usually does so symmetrically.

8.8 How Much in Residual Income Can I Expect?

The model generates residual income when the sum of all the sell trades surpasses the sum of the buy trades. When the cash draw has been completely offset, a surplus is generated.

The residual income amount depends on how many opportunities the market has presented for both the buy and sell trades. In a relatively "quiet" market, more sell trades will likely be triggered, while in a volatile period more buy trades are likely. Over a long period of time, with a variety of conditions, they could become mostly balanced, in which case the account will be left with the extra gains resulting from buying at the lows and selling at the highs.

Additionally, adjusting the multipliers that control the buy and sell amounts will affect this balance as well.

8.9 Paper Trading

Paper trading, also known as simulated trading or virtual trading, is a method for investors and traders to practice buying and selling financial assets without risking real money. It's essentially a risk-free training ground that replicates the live market environment using virtual funds and real market data.

To paper trade, enter your simulated positions into the model and follow the action without actually executing any real trades. When a trade alert comes in, add or subtract shares as suggested. When ready to start real money trading, delete the virtual positions and enter the real ones.

8.10 Extending the Model Beyond ETFs

The concept presented here makes our model growth-oriented, diversified and streamlined, freeing us from the cherry-picking work and constant maintenance required for individual stock holdings. It also greatly simplifies the buying and selling under the model. On the other hand, we may be giving up on participating more actively in a possible run-up of many individual stocks. However, it's hard to know in advance which ones will enjoy this and by how much. It is always a good idea to remain diversified.

Adding individual stocks to the portfolio is possible, although with some caveats. First, each addition should come with appropriate research, or "fundamental analysis"[63], building a good understanding of the business, its risks, and future prospects. Second, there should be a good mix of sector leaders and smaller players. The amount of exposure taken on each name should reflect its risk-return profile relative to the others and should be adjusted as needed. Finally, regular tracking of the news, financials, and price performance is essential, as is buying and selling when appropriate while keeping the portfolio in proper balance.

Investing in individual stocks is outside the scope of this guidebook. The author is, however, already managing portfolios of stocks, ETFs and cryptocurrencies, and can share with the readers some of his experience. More information on this will be posted on the website.

8.11 The ETF4Life Website

The **ETF4Life** website[64] and investment assistance tools were created to help users enhance their portfolio's long-term performance by following the concepts laid out in this book.

Tutorials for setting up the tools are included within each of them.

- To protect your financial security, our app will **never** ask for your brokerage account information.

8.12 Conclusion: The Long Game

The stock market is a machine that rewards patience and penalizes impulse. By adopting the "supervised autopilot" approach, you have moved beyond the noise of daily fluctuations and into a disciplined, engineering-grade framework for wealth accumulation. You now understand that volatility is not a risk to be feared, but a friend to be leveraged.

Success in this model does not require you to be a company insider or a high-frequency trader; it requires the discipline to follow the trendlines and the confidence to act when the herd panics . As you move from the pages of this book into the execution of your own portfolio, remember that the goal is not a "get rich quick" result, but a sustained, long-term growth trajectory .

The tools and strategies provided here are your roadmap. Now, it is time to take the wheel.

Next Steps Checklist

To ensure you start your journey with the same precision described in this guide, follow this final checklist:

1. Choose Your Brokerage: Ensure your account allows for dollar-based or fractional share trading.

2. Define Your Reserves: Decide on your initial cash allocation based on the current NASDAQ trendline position.

3. Place initial trades with your brokerage.

4. Activate the Engine: Visit https://etf4life.app/ to update your holdings, set up your portfolio weights and start receiving trade alerts .

- **The explanations in the next sections are merely attempted at what's necessary to understand the concepts behind the terminology**. More information can be found by searching online or by tuning-in to business-related broadcasts such as CNBC, Fox Business Network or Bloomberg TV

Appendix A: Market and Economic Topics

A.1 Technical Vs Fundamental Analysis

Technical analysis and fundamental analysis are two distinct approaches to evaluating stocks. Fundamental analysis focuses on a company's intrinsic value by examining financial statements, economic indicators, and qualitative factors like management quality and industry trends. It seeks to understand a company's underlying health and future prospects, typically favored by long-term investors. In contrast, technical analysis relies on historical price and volume data, using charts and indicators to identify patterns and predict future price movements, often appealing to short-term traders. While **fundamental** analysis digs into **"why"** a stock might perform, **technical** analysis focuses on **"when"** to buy or sell based on market sentiment reflected in price action.

A.2 Market Indices

S&P 500: The Standard & Poor's 500, is a stock market index that tracks the performance of 500 of the largest publicly traded companies in the United States. It's widely considered a strong indicator of the overall health of the U.S. stock market and economy. The S&P 500 is a capitalization-weighted index, meaning companies with larger market values have a greater impact on the index's performance.

NASDAQ: The NASDAQ Composite Index is a stock market index that includes almost all stocks listed on the Nasdaq stock exchange, on which several stock sectors are traded with a special focus on technology stocks. It is a market capitalization-weighted index.

NASDAQ-100: A stock market index made up of equity securities issued by 100 of the largest non-financial companies listed on the Nasdaq stock exchange. Similar to the S&P 500 and NASDAQ Composite, it's a market-cap weighted index. This means companies with larger market values have a greater influence on the index's movement. However, it's "modified" in that it has rules to cap the influence of the very largest components, preventing any single stock from dominating too much. This helps maintain a degree of diversification within the top holdings.

The Dow: The DJIA (Dow Jones Industrial Average) tracks the performance of 30 "blue-chip" companies, which are generally large, well-established, and financially stable publicly traded companies in the U.S. Unlike the S&P 500 and NASDAQ Composite, which are market-capitalization weighted, the DJIA is a price-weighted index. This means that companies with higher stock prices have a greater influence on the index's value, regardless of their total market capitalization.

Russel 2000: The Russell 2000 Index tracks the performance of approximately 2,000 small-capitalization (small-cap) companies in the U.S. It's a subset of the broader Russell 3000 Index, which aims to represent about 98% of the investable U.S. equity market.

Like the S&P 500 and the NASDAQ, the Russell 2000 is capitalization-weighted.

A.3 Market Capitalization

Also known as "market cap", it's a measure of a company's total value based on its outstanding shares of stock. It is calculated by multiplying the stock price by the number of shares outstanding.

Small-cap stocks: generally $300 million to $2 billion in market cap, belong to younger, less established companies. While these carry the highest risk and volatility due to their sensitivity to economic shifts and limited resources, they also offer the greatest potential for rapid, outsized growth if successful, appealing to investors with a higher risk tolerance and a longer investment horizon.

Mid-cap stocks: typically $2 billion to $10 billion in market cap, offer a balance between growth and stability; they are often companies in an expansion phase, providing higher growth potential than large-caps but with more volatility.

Large-cap stocks: generally over $10 billion in market cap, representing established and often globally recognized companies, are typically less volatile and offer more stable, though slower, growth than smaller cap stocks. They are favored by risk-averse investors seeking consistent returns and often dividend payments.

Mega-cap stocks are the equities of the largest publicly traded companies in the world, distinguished by their enormous market capitalization. They represent the top tier of the market and have an outsized influence on major stock indices like the S&P 500. While there is no single official definition, a mega-cap stock is generally defined as a company with a market capitalization of $200 billion or more.

A.4 Growth Vs Value Stocks

Growth stocks represent companies expected to expand their earnings and revenue at a faster rate than the overall market, often reinvesting profits back into the business rather than paying dividends. These companies typically have high price-to-earnings (P/E) ratios, reflecting investor optimism about their future potential, and are common in innovative sectors like technology. Conversely, value stocks are those trading below their intrinsic worth, often due to temporary setbacks or market skepticism, and are characterized by lower P/E ratios and a tendency to pay dividends. While growth stocks offer higher capital appreciation potential but also greater volatility, value stocks tend to be more stable and provide income, making them appealing to different investor risk appetites and time horizons.

A.5 Time Value of Money

The concept that a sum of money is worth more today than the same sum will be worth at a future date due to its earnings potential in the interim. In other words, a dollar received today is worth more than a dollar received in the future.

A.6 Efficient Market Hypothesis (EMH)

The EMH asserts that asset prices, particularly stocks, fully reflect all available information at any given time. This means it is impossible to consistently earn returns above the overall market average, once adjusted for risk, through strategies like stock picking or market timing. Prices only change in response to new, unpredictable information.

EMH assertions are challenged by market anomalies, such as bubbles, crashes, irrational behavior, certain documented effects and some outperforming investors.

A.7 Gross Domestic Product (GDP)

GDP is a key measure of a country's economic output, representing the total monetary value of all goods and services produced within its borders during a specific time period, typically a year. It's a fundamental indicator used to gauge the size and growth rate of an economy.

A.8 Smart Money / Dumb Money

The terms "smart money" and "dumb money" are used in financial markets to distinguish between different types of investors and their perceived levels of sophistication and success. **Smart money** generally refers to the capital controlled by institutional investors, hedge funds, central banks, and other financial professionals. These participants are believed to have superior resources, extensive research capabilities, access to proprietary data, and a deeper understanding of market dynamics. They often engage in in-depth fundamental and technical analysis, exhibit disciplined investment strategies, and tend to have longer-term investment horizons. Their large-scale movements can significantly influence market trends, and their trading activity is often tracked by retail investors for potential insights. **Dumb money**, conversely, typically refers to individual or retail investors who may lack the extensive resources, experience, or analytical tools of their institutional counterparts. This group is often characterized by emotional decision-making, trend-chasing, and a tendency to react to news or hype. They may buy assets when prices are rising (FOMO - fear of missing out) and sell when prices are falling (panic selling), often leading to suboptimal returns. While the terms can seem derogatory, they are meant to describe behavioral patterns rather than individual intelligence. The GameStop short squeeze, for instance, is a notable example where a collective of "dumb money" retail investors successfully challenged "smart money" hedge funds.

A.9 Stock Valuations

Stock valuation is the process of determining the theoretical or "intrinsic" value of a company's stock. This is a crucial step for investors to decide whether a stock is currently overvalued, undervalued, or fairly valued in the market. One of the most common is the Price-to-Earnings (P/E) ratio. It is calculated by dividing a company's current share price by its earnings per share (EPS). The P/E ratio essentially tells you how much investors are willing to pay for each dollar of a company's earnings. A high P/E might suggest investors expect strong future growth, while a low P/E could indicate the stock is undervalued or that investors have concerns about its prospects. It's most useful when comparing a company's P/E to its historical average or to the P/E ratios of comparable companies in the same industry.

A.10 Valuation Bubbles

Also known as an asset bubble or economic bubble, occurs when the collective price of an asset class, such as stocks, real estate, or commodities, rises significantly and rapidly to levels that far exceed its intrinsic or fundamental value. This disconnect means the price is not justified by the underlying financial health, earnings, or future prospects of the asset class.

A.11 Brokerage Firms

To execute trades under this model, it is better to use a brokerage firm that offers dollar-based trading (as opposed to whole share-based). Several firms offer this feature; Robinhood is a good example for such a firm. Others include Interactive Brokers and SoFi. Some firms, however, offer this feature under a separate trade category (such as fractional shares), which could be somewhat inconvenient.

A.12 Quantitative Easing and Tightening

Quantitative Easing (QE) and **Quantitative Tightening (QT)** are opposite monetary policies used by central banks (like the U.S. Federal Reserve) to influence the economy, primarily by adjusting the money supply and long-term interest rates. **QE is stimulus** (pumping money in) and **QT is restraint** (sucking money out).

Appendix B: Financial and Trading Terminology

B.1 Volatility

Stock market volatility refers to the degree and frequency with which a stock or market index price moves up or down over a period of time. It reflects the uncertainty or risk associated with the price fluctuations of a particular investment or the overall market. While volatility can be both positive and negative, investors tend to be more concerned about downside volatility, which can lead to market corrections or bear markets.

B.2 Diversification

Portfolio diversification is an investment strategy that involves mixing a wide variety of investments within a portfolio. The core idea is to reduce the overall risk of an investment portfolio by spreading investments across different asset classes, industries, and geographic regions. By diversifying, you aim to limit your exposure to any single investment type and potentially offset the poor performance of one investment with the better performance of another.

B.3 Liquidity

The ease and speed with which a stock or other security can be bought or sold without significantly affecting its market price. Large-cap stocks and ETFs are generally highly liquid, while small-cap stocks, penny stocks, or shares of companies traded on less active exchanges may be less liquid.

B.4 Correlation

A statistical measure that quantifies the degree to which the prices of two or more stocks, or other financial assets, move in relation to each other. It helps investors understand how different investments behave in response to market events and economic conditions.

B.5 Productivity

Productivity is the ratio of output to inputs. When an economy produces more goods and services with the same amount of resources, or the same amount of goods and services with fewer resources, productivity has increased. It is a crucial concept that underpins long-term economic growth and improvements in living standards.

B.6 Implied Volatility

A crucial concept, particularly relevant to **options trading**. It's a forward-looking measure that represents the market's collective expectation of how much the price of an underlying asset (like a stock or an index) will move in the future.

B.7 Drawdowns

The decline in the value of an investment or portfolio from its peak to its subsequent trough (lowest point). It's a key metric for assessing risk and volatility, particularly during market downturns. Drawdown is often expressed as a percentage, calculated by dividing the difference between the peak and trough values by the peak value.

B.8 "Yield Trap"

The dividend yield of a dividend-issuing stock is calculated by dividing the annual dividend by the stock's current price. A high yield can be a warning sign. It often indicates that the stock's price has fallen significantly due to underlying business problems, while the dividend has not yet been cut. Investors who chase these high yields may inadvertently be buying into a troubled company that is at high risk of a dividend cut and further price declines.

B.9 Tracking Error

Tracking error is a measure of the risk that an investment portfolio's performance will deviate from the performance of its chosen **benchmark index** (like the S&P 500).

It essentially quantifies **how closely a portfolio follows the index** it is designed to track, making it a critical metric for passive investments like index funds and Exchange-Traded Funds (ETFs). The lower the tracking error, the more accurately the fund is replicating the returns of its benchmark.

B.10 Financial Leverage

Financial leverage is a strategy where a company or investor uses **borrowed money (debt)** to finance the purchase of assets or an investment.

The goal is to increase the potential returns (profit or capital gain) on the investment. It works by having the **return on the asset exceed the cost of borrowing** (interest payments).

A common example for individuals is taking out a **mortgage** to buy a home. You use a small down payment (equity) and a large loan (debt) to control a high-value asset.

Appendix C: How-To Guides

C.1 Portfolio Management in Excel

Key Excel Features

The core feature for building a live-updating stock portfolio is the **Stocks Data Type**.

- **Availability**: This feature is available for users of Excel for Microsoft 365 and Excel for the web.
- **Functionality**: It automatically retrieves current stock prices, market capitalization, daily changes, and other relevant information directly from linked online sources. Data typically updates once per day after the market closes or can be manually refreshed.

Step-by-Step Guide

Here are the basic steps to create a simple stock portfolio:

1. **Set Up Your Workbook**: Open a new blank workbook in Excel. In the first sheet, create columns with headers such

as "Ticker Symbol", "Company Name", "Shares Purchased", "Purchase Price", "Initial Investment", "Current Price", "Current Value", and "Gain/Loss".

2. **Enter Ticker Symbols**: In the "Ticker Symbol" column, list the companies you hold (e.g., AAPL, GOOG, TSLA).

3. **Convert to Stocks Data Type**:
   1. Select the cells containing your ticker symbols.
   2. Go to the **Data** tab in the ribbon.
   3. Click on the **Stocks** button (under the Data Types section). Excel will convert the text entries into recognized "Stock" entities, often showing a small stock icon in the cell.

4. **Extract Data**:
   1. Select any cell that has been converted to a stock data type. A small icon will appear next to it.
   2. Click the icon to see a dropdown list of available data fields (e.g., Price, Market Cap, 52-week high, Industry, etc.).
   3. Select "Price" to populate the "Current Price" column for all your stocks automatically.

5. **Add Your Investment Data**: Manually input the number of shares you purchased and the price you paid per share into their respective columns.

6. **Calculate Values and Performance**: Use formulas to manage your data:
   1. **Initial Investment**: = [Shares Purchased] * [Purchase Price]
   2. **Current Value**: = [Shares Purchased] * [Current Price]
   3. **Gain/Loss**: = [Current Value] - [Initial Investment]

7. **Visualize and Analyze**: Use conditional formatting to visually highlight gains (e.g., green) and losses (e.g., red). You can also insert charts and pivot tables to visualize your portfolio's allocation by sector or market cap.

For more advanced features like automatic data refresh using VBA code or portfolio optimization using the Solver tool, numerous tutorials are available from the Excel community on platforms like YouTube.

C.2 Trendlines in Excel

The app calculates the NASDAQ trendline on a daily basis. If you prefer to create one on your own, an Excel spreadsheet may be useful for that.

1. Open an Excel spreadsheet.
2. Get the data: go to Nasdaq.com and enter COMP in the "search for a symbol" field, then click on "NASDAQ Composite Index" in the dropdown.
3. Click on "Max" to capture the full multi-year history, and then click to download the .CSV file.
4. Open the file and save as Excel Workbook.
5. Sort the data: select the columns, click on ""Sort & Filter" in the ribbon and select "Sort Oldest to Newest".
6. Select the Date and Close/Last columns.
7. In the ribbon, select Insert, then click on the line chart type in the Charts box and select the first 2-D line option.
8. The historical chart is now inserted into the worksheet. You may move it to a new sheet under the same workbook: right-click, Move Chart, New Sheet.

9. In the new sheet, right-click on the graph and select Add Trendline.

10. Select Exponential. The trendline will be built over the graph.

- Note that an exponential trendline would apply to a large historical period of the index but may not fit shorter intervals.

C.3 Model Self-Management

Here are the guidelines in case you chose to set the model up and manage it on your own.

Note: threshold values are suggested based on a specific historical simulation. The app may optimize them occasionally based on recent market data.

1. Follow the steps listed in Chapter 8 to open a trading account, set up a budgetary cash reserve, select and fund the portfolio positions. Make sure to assign a percentage weight to each position and to track the portfolio net gain.

2. After building the trendline as described in the previous segment, update the NASDAQ historical data series daily (and intraday) and let Excel calculate the new trendline value each time using the statistical formula LOGEST.

3. Set up and track the following list of trade indicators on a daily basis:

    1. **Buy Indicators**

        1. VIX intraday price: if higher than 30, mark as "triggered".

2. NASDAQ Composite Index daily change: if negative, mark "triggered".
3. Trendline Offset (a percentage value of where the NASDAQ price is in relation to the trendline value): if below 6%, mark "triggered".
4. NASDAQ drop from its most recent record high: if below -20%, mark "triggered".
5. A trade alert is active when all the above 4 Buy indicators are triggered together.
6. When a Buy alert is active, use the reserves to increase the portfolio value by 1.5%.
7. From this total amount, calculate the purchase amount for each position based on its assigned weight. This is the suggested amount to buy for that security.

2. **Sell Indicators**
   1. Portfolio net gain: if greater than 20%, mark as "triggered".
   2. Trendline Offset: if greater than 0%, mark as "triggered".
   3. NASDAQ intraday price: if at a new record high, mark "triggered".
   4. Portfolio Net Gain value change since last Sell trade: if greater than $500, mark "triggered".
   5. A trade alert is active when all the above 4 Sell indicators are triggered together.
   6. When a Sell alert is active, exercise 30% of the portfolio daily value rise.
   7. From this amount, calculate the Sell amount for each position based on its assigned weight. This is the suggested amount to sell for that security.

Appendix D: Full Legal Disclosure

Full Legal Disclosure and Risk Warning

The information presented in this guidebook, including all charts, tables, strategies, and discussions of Exchange-Transposed Funds (ETFs) and market trends, is for educational purposes only and is provided *"as is"* without warranty of any kind.

(Investment Risk Disclaimer and Professional Advice Disclaimer remain the same as previously provided.)

App and Technology Disclosure

1. **RELATIONSHIP AND FUNCTION:** The companion application (the "App") in its **online and downloadable form**, is provided as an **optional, non-essential educational supplement** to this book, intended strictly for practicing the methodologies discussed herein. The App is a **simulation tool** and its functionality is limited to theoretical application and record-keeping, not real-time, live investment execution.

2. **NO SOLICITATION OR RECOMMENDATION:** Neither this guidebook nor the App constitutes a solicitation, recommendation, or offer to buy or sell any specific ETF, security, or financial instrument. The App does **not** evaluate a user's suitability, risk tolerance, or financial situation, and any output or "score" it provides is for **simulated, theoretical evaluation only. Trade alerts** are designed as a market-wide, portfolio-level timing signal and not a recommendation to buy or sell a specific security. **Portfolio positions** are selected and traded by the users, where selection rules may fit many different ETFs as explained in the text. The App **does not execute trades** on behalf of its users.

3. **TECHNOLOGY RISK:** The accuracy and availability of the App are subject to factors outside the control of the author and publisher, including software bugs, data feed errors, and device compatibility issues. The author and publisher **expressly disclaim all liability** for any data inaccuracy, service interruption, or technical malfunction arising from the use of the App.

4. **SEPARATE TERMS OF USE:** Use of the App is governed by its own independent **Terms of Use** and **Privacy Policy,** which the user must accept upon signup. These policies may contain additional disclaimers regarding data, liability, and software performance. The terms of the App are entirely separate from the terms and liability limitations of this book.

About the Author

Warren Sterling is a retired computer engineering manager and Silicon Valley veteran who has spent decades at the forefront of technological innovation. Throughout his career in the heart of the tech industry, he witnessed firsthand the disruptive power of engineering and the massive wealth creation driven by the technology sector . This background provided him with a unique perspective: the most reliable growth in the modern economy isn't found in guessing the next "hot" stock, but in understanding the inherent, exponential trajectory of the industries that power our world .

Upon retiring, Sterling noticed a critical gap in traditional financial planning. Most retail investors were either paralyzed by market volatility or making emotional decisions that undermined their long-term success . Applying the same analytical precision required in computer engineering, he developed a quantitative investment model designed to remove human bias from the equation .

Sterling is the founder of **ETF4Life**, where he developed a suite of investment assistant tools—including web-based applications and Excel-driven models—that function as a "supervised autopilot" for the individual investor . His contrarian strategy focuses on identifying market extremes using technical indicators like the NASDAQ trendline and the VIX "fear gauge" to turn market stress into growth opportunities .

Today, Sterling remains an active portfolio manager, overseeing diversified assets across stocks, ETFs, and cryptocurrencies. Through his writing and tools, he aims to empower investors of all ages to move past the "noise" of the daily news cycle and adopt a disciplined, engineering-grade approach to lifelong financial security .

Connect with the Model: To access the trade-alert engine, downloadable Excel tools, and the latest model updates, visit: **https://etf4life.app/**.

Endnotes

1. etf4life.app/about
2. Etf4life.app/
3. Appendix B.1
4. Appendix B.2
5. Chapter 8.9
6. Appendix B.1
7. Appendix B.2
8. Chapter 7.1
9. Chapter 7.1
10. Chapter 3.2
11. Chapter 3.2
12. Appendix A.1
13. Chapter 3.3
14. Chapter 2.7
15. Appendix B.10
16. Appendix A.2
17. Appendix B.9
18. Appendix B.8
19. Appendix B.6
20. Appendix A.1
21. Appendix A.6
22. Appendix A.7

23.   Appendix A.8
24.   Appendix A.9
25.   Appendix A.10
26.   www.cnn.com/markets/fear-and-greed
27.   Appendix A.5
28.   Appendix A.1
29.   Chapter 4.2
30.   Chapter 1.4
31.   Chapter 2.7
32.   Chapter 8.11
33.   www.invesco.com/qqq-etf/en/home.html
34.   Appendix A.2
35.   Appendix A.3
36.   www.sectorspdrs.com/mainfund/XLK
37.   Appendix A.4
38.   www.ssga.com/us/en/intermediary/etfs/state-street-spdr-sp-500-etf-trust-spy
39.   Appendix A.2
40.   www.ishares.com/us/products/239710/ishares-russell-2000-etf
41.   Appendix A.2
42.   Appendix B.5
43.   tinyurl.com/yc2e8zus
44.   amplifyetfs.com/hack/
45.   https://www.wisdomtree.com/investments/etfs/mega-trends/wcld
46.   procureetfs.com/ufo/
47.   www.ishares.com/us/products/239502/ishares-us-aerospace-defense-etf
48.   www.ishares.com/us/products/239771/ishares-north-americantechsoftware-etf

49. tinyurl.com/5x5ankmz

50. tinyurl.com/3vepj635

51. Appendix 8.11

52. tradingeconomics.com/calendar

53. www.investing.com/economic-calendar/

54. www.briefing.com/calendars/economic?Filter=All

55. Appendix A.10

56. Appendix A.11

57. Chapter 2.4

58. Chapter 4.2

59. Chapter 5.4

60. Chapter 5.7

61. Chapter 2.11

62. Chapter 3.3

63. Appendix A.1

64. www.etf4life.app